ZEBULON PIKE

The Life and Times of an Adventurer

ZEBULON PIKE

=

*The Life and Times of
an Adventurer*

JOHN UPTON TERRELL

Weybright and Talley
NEW YORK

To Donna

who never needed to climb Pike's Peak
to see a far horizon

© *by John Upton Terrell 1968*

Published in the United States by
WEYBRIGHT AND TALLEY, INC.
3 East 54th Street,
New York, N.Y. 10022

Library of Congress Catalog Card No. 68–12871

PRINTED IN THE UNITED STATES OF AMERICA

ZEBULON PIKE

The Life and Times of an Adventurer

1

LIEUTENANT ZEBULON MONTGOMERY PIKE was twenty-seven years old when he received the orders launching him upon a brief but glamorous career of espionage, intrigue, and adventure that would make him a controversial national figure for the remainder of his life.

At St. Louis, early in May, 1806, he was directed to prepare for an expedition to the western mountains, "approximate to the settlements of New Mexico," for the purpose of exploring and determining the locations of the upper reaches of the Arkansas and Red Rivers.

The orders were issued, at first verbally and later in writing, by General James Wilkinson, who not only held the two highest offices in Louisiana Territory—Governor and Commander in Chief of American military forces—but also was a secret agent in the service of the Spanish Government, an avocation that on several past occasions had been very profitable to him.

No army officer or government official stationed on the frontier in the spring of 1806, least of all Lieutenant Pike, who had lived there since early boyhood, could have failed to realize the significance and importance of the assignment. Relations between Spain and the United States had deteriorated to the point where a complete break appeared inevitable. The movement of an American force, no matter how small and regardless of its mission, would be viewed by the Spanish as a threat to their security, if not as an overt act of aggression against the domain of His Catholic Majesty.

Louisiana Territory had belonged to the United States only three years. During that period, all efforts to define its boundaries had failed. Indeed, the prospects of reconciling the conflicting claims of Spain and the Washington government appeared less promising than they had been at any time since negotiations had begun. In the South, conditions were reaching a critical stage, with Spanish and American troops prepared to shoot at each other.

Spanish intelligence was swift, and, in view of the circumstances under which it was obliged to function, its high levels of accuracy and efficiency were hardly less than remarkable.

Long before Pike had received written orders for the western expedition, Spanish agents in St. Louis had sent a report about it, *urgente y secreto*, to the seat of government for the northern Spanish provinces, Chihuahua City. The dispatch had been addressed to General Don Nimesio Salcedo, who, like Wilkinson, occupied the two posts of Governor and Commander in Chief of the armed forces.

It was a good 2,300 miles from St. Louis to Chihuahua City. The only reasonably safe route for a courier was down the Mississippi to the vicinity of Natchez, west to Natchitoches, on to the mission town of Nacogdoches, southwest to San Antonio, the headquarters for Texas, through the vast sweeps of chaparral to the Rio Grande, and across the immense, rough, barren ranges of northern Mexico.

No Spanish agent in St. Louis at the time would have given a moment's thought to attempting a passage across the Great Plains and mountains to Santa Fe. The old Camino Real, from the New Mexico capital to El Paso del Norte and Chihuahua, was, of course, safe enough; it was traveled regularly by troops and trade caravans. But to reach Santa Fe involved a horseback journey of more than twelve hundred miles through country that, although not completely unknown, contained no trading posts or missions that might have been used as havens, no reliable allies, and that was inhabited by red savages whose attitude toward a white messenger would have been far less difficult to predict than the weather. Yet, that was the route Pike would take.

At Natchez, the important dispatch to Governor Salcedo passed through the hands of the Spanish consul, Captain Stephen Minor, and there its chances of remaining secret became, at best, extremely poor. Minor was an American defector who had become a Spanish subject. His sworn allegiance to a foreign power, however, did not inspire any feeling of loyalty to it; that would not have been in keeping with either his character or the pattern of his past life. An old and close friend of General Wilkinson, he had not only operated with him in espionage activities against the United States but had long shared with him a dream of overthrowing the Spanish provincial government in North America, which he had taken an oath to support and defend.

However, Minor did not delay the message. He sent it on to Captain Sebastian Rodriguez at Nacogdoches, who forwarded it to Colonel Antonio Cordero, the chief officer of the Province of Texas, at San Antonio. From that place it was transmitted to its destination, Salcedo's desk. And the Governor, fully aware of its urgency, made copies and sent them in three directions with all possible speed—to Mexico City, to the Spanish Minister in Washington, and to the Foreign Office in Spain.

The intelligence left no doubts that if Pike carried out his instructions, he would enter Spanish regions south of the disputed northern boundary of Louisiana Territory. Governor Salcedo and every other high-ranking Spanish official apprised of it realized at once that the American expedition would be an incursion that must not be permitted to occur.

Precedent and experience guided their reasoning. They had known years of diplomatic strain and territorial contention, and very little (it might be said, none) of the high level wrangling and maneuvering had brought results favorable to their country.

Since the birth of the United States, American settlement west of the Alleghenies had pressed with steadily mounting force against their borders, creating economic, political, and legal issues that had proved to be insoluble by either negotiation or treaty. It had long before become obvious that Americans were not to be halted in their migrations to the West, certainly not by any lawful means, and most probably not even by threats of armed reprisals. With the admission of Kentucky and Tennessee as states of the Union, the possibility (which had existed for a time) of those areas entering a separate alliance with Spain was forever gone.

The Spanish Crown, at last, had seen only one way to resolve the dilemma: create a barrier between its American provinces and the United States. On October 1, 1800, Louisiana in its entirety was ceded secretly to France. Spain believed that by this move it had freed itself of the menace of American penetration. How wrong that belief was had soon become apparent.

President Jefferson considered France far more dangerous than Spain as a western neighbor. He was fully informed of Napoleon's ambition to build a powerful colonial empire in the North American West, and he knew that the daring and unpredictable Corsican might well close the Mississippi permanently to all but French commerce. If that happened, it would bring political disorders in the western areas of the United States that would be beyond the means of the Washington government to control. Jefferson sent emissaries to Paris in the hope of gaining assurance from Napoleon that no such drastic move was contemplated.

But European political changes, not negotiations, solved the problem. Napoleon's dream of a colonial empire had been shattered. He offered to sell Louisiana Territory to the United States. A price of 15 million dollars, the greatest real estate bargain in all the history of the world, was agreed upon, and the transaction was consummated on April 30, 1803.

Staggered by the blow, Spain found herself once

more confronted by all the problems that resulted from being immediately to the west of the dynamic and growing United States and also plagued by a major question that had not previously existed: location of the remote Louisiana Territory boundaries.

Complicating the situation was the presence in the center of the frontier stage of a man who had long played leading roles in western dramas, General James Wilkinson of the American Army. But if the Spanish had no explanation for Wilkinson's previous unconscionable actions and no illusions about his character, neither did they have any alternative but to keep him on the payroll while at the same time attempting to thwart his schemes. Exposing him would have done no good, and in all probability, charges against him would not have been accepted by the American government. Moreover, a refusal to associate with him might well prevent them from knowing anything at all of what he was doing or planning. As long as he remained in their service, their agents would be able to keep in contact with him and to keep him under surveillance.

A good example of the desirability of retaining such a source of information was the projected Pike Expedition. How many dispatches about it followed the first message from St. Louis to Governor Salcedo is not a matter of historical record. Whatever the number, and there must have been a good many, they vanished into the jungle of Spanish military and diplomatic archives and undoubtedly will remain there forever. But if their precise wording cannot be repeated, ensuing events and later correspondence make their content and their purport unmistakably clear. They illustrated a case of spies spying on spies. And they stressed these factors:

Inasmuch as the Pike Expedition had been ordered by General Wilkinson, it would be logical to assume that it had been authorized by the Secretary of War, Henry Dearborn, if not by President Jefferson. But in view of Wilkinson's past record of defying his superiors, such an assumption could well be erroneous.

The company to be sent out would be disguised as either a trading or a scientific mission, possibly as both; but in fact its members would be (with two exceptions) soldiers of the regular American Army.

Pike was a young but enterprising and capable officer in line for a captaincy. He had recently won some distinction as an explorer of the Upper Mississippi. He had led a military company to that region—also on orders from Wilkinson, but without official sanction of either the War Department or the President—purportedly to discover the headwaters of the great river. But Governor Salcedo should consider the suggestion that Pike's actual mission to the Upper Mississippi had been to report on the activities of British fur traders and to open the way for halting their operations in areas claimed by the United States. Governor Wilkinson himself was very much interested in the developing fur trade and was associated with St. Louis traders, notably the prominent Chouteaus.

The two members of the Pike company without military rank would be a Dr. John Hamilton Robinson, a civilian surgeon who had appeared in St. Louis in 1805, and A. F. Baronet Vasquez, an Indian trader and trapper, who would act as interpreter. Both were known to be confidants of General Wilkinson.

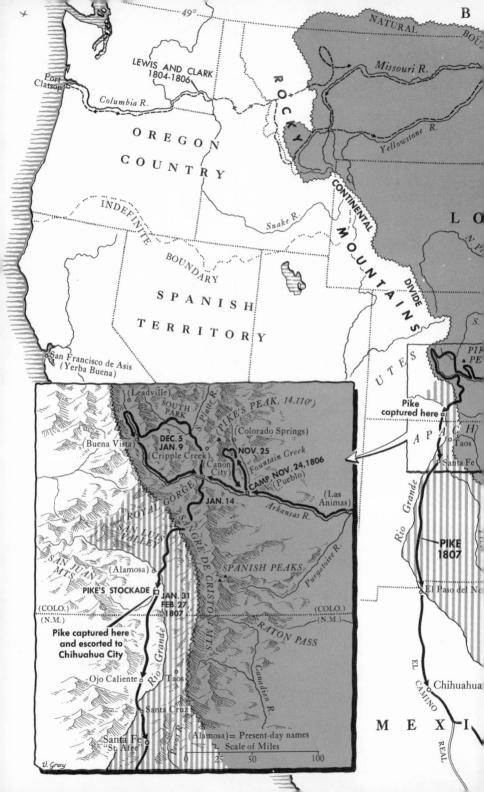

JOURNEYS OF
ZEBULON PIKE
1805-1807

········· Present-day boundaries
Scale of Miles

0   100   200   300

There was *no* evidence at hand in St. Louis to indicate that Pike's western tour of duty was not primarily for the purpose of ascertaining the strength of Spanish defenses along the Louisiana Territory borders, as a preliminary step toward a contemplated full-scale offensive to acquire Spanish territory.

There *was* evidence showing that General Wilkinson's extracurricular and surreptitious activities were known to officials in Washington. Why he had, under such circumstances, been appointed to his two high offices was a question not easily answered. But any attempt to explain the motives of Americans, or the complexities of their political system, could be expected to be unproductive.

It might be helpful if Governor Salcedo would recall the name of Aaron Burr and the activities menacing the Spanish provinces that had been conducted under his aegis. Nor should it be forgotten that Burr, Vice-President of the United States from 1801 to 1805, had long been Wilkinson's close associate. Burr's own treasonous activities were the subject of official documents. Even while he schemed with Wilkinson to destroy Spanish power in New Mexico and Texas and to establish an imperial dynasty (with himself on the throne) in Mexico proper, he attempted to extort money from both the British and Spanish Ministers at the American seat of government, the Honorable Anthony Merry, and the Marques de Casa, Carlos Martinez Yrujo. To neither of these distinguished gentlemen had Burr disclosed his true plan, although they had suspected its nature. Indeed, he had sought to play their respective influences one against the other by making a dishonest recital to each of them.

Governor Salcedo should be apprised that Burr and Wilkinson were at the moment in close communication with each other, outside of the ordinary Government channels. Furthermore, it appeared obvious not only that they were continuing to conspire against Spain but that Burr was fully informed of the plan to send Pike into Spanish territory and had endorsed Wilkinson's machinations.

The analyses and deductions of the Spanish agents in St. Louis, if incomplete and vague in some respects, were remarkably shrewd. Certain aspects of the Pike expedition justifiably puzzled them. These pertained for the most part to its timing, its size, and its members.

For at least a century, Spanish traders from Santa Fe had traveled spasmodically along the eastern slope of the northern Rocky Mountains. In this period, or even before it, soldiers had been sent in pursuit of Pueblo Indians who had sought escape from slavery in mines and on ranchos by fleeing northward. There had been numerous organized chases of this kind, and although the identities of most of the pursuers had been forgotten, some were well remembered. These ventures comprised a history that Pike would have done well to study. It was available to him, for there were traders in St. Louis who were familiar with it. Perhaps he did acquire some knowledge of it, but if that were so, he would choose to ignore what he had learned at the time when it would have been most useful to him.

He might have found out, for example, that as long ago as the 1670s, Don Juan Archuleta had led twenty *soldados* after some Taos Indians who had slipped away when ordered by a *padre* to build a parish church without compensation. Archuleta had traveled over Palo Flechado Pass, through the Sangre de Christo Range, and over Raton Pass to the Purgatoire. Somewhere on the plains immediately east of the mountains [eastern Colorado] he overtook the runaways and brought them back to Taos. The place of the capture was in an area known as El Cuartelejo [Far Quarter].

Spanish traders and slave hunters had not only come to know the Indians living in this region but had come into contact with other peoples on the Canadian, the Cimarron, the Arkansas, and the North and South Platte Rivers. At the close of the seventeenth century, they had made an alarming discovery. Among some of these tribes (notably the Apaches), they found powder flasks, sword belts, buckles, decorated waistcoats, shoes, and ironware cooking pots that were of French origin—all products competitive with Spanish trade. The possessors of these objects claimed they were obtained in fights with the Pawnees, and the Pawnees lived on the Platte River. The questions which troubled the sleep of Spanish officials were: Had the Pawnees obtained the goods directly from the French or from other tribes inhabiting country farther north and east that had been penetrated by French *voyageurs?* Had the Apaches actually met the French farther to the south than the Platte, perhaps on the plains bordering the Canadian?

There was only one way to obtain answers to these questions. The task had been given to Captain Juan de Ulibarri, and in the early summer of 1706, he set out from Taos with a well equipped force of one hundred and forty men. While his principal duty was to determine how far the French had invaded Spanish territory, he was also instructed to make a show of force before any Indians he encountered and to warn them that attacks on Spanish settlements would result in their annihilation. An additional assignment was to bring back several hundred Picuris who had fled their pueblo and were believed to have taken refuge among Jicarillas on the Arkansas River.

Ulibarri's route would have been of particular interest to Pike. It had been Ulibarri's plan to follow the customary trail to El Cuartelejo. But before reaching Raton Pass, he had turned north when his scouts reported that Comanches were waiting in strength for him. Wisely, he did not attempt to make a show of force for the benefit of Indians lying in ambush in a mountain defile.

Reaching the upper Purgatoire by another route, Ulibarri turned northwest, crossing the Apishapa River. To his left stood the magnificent Spanish Peaks. From the Huerfano River, he went on to the Arkansas, striking it opposite the mouth of Fountain Creek. Here he rested his column.

Against the sky toward the northwest, a great snow-capped peak was clearly visible. In the year 1706, Ulibarri had no name for it. A century later, in the year 1806, the Spanish did not dream that this immense mountain would soon be known to the world as Pikes Peak.

Ulibarri found the escaped Picuris and persuaded them to return to their homeland. But more important was his discovery of indisputable evidence that the French were not far away. He found a new French gun in the possession of a Picuri chief. It had been purchased from Pawnees near the place where the waters of the Platte divided. There could be no doubt that it had not been in

[13]

the possession of the Pawnees for any length of time. And the place where the Platte split into its northern and southern branches was less than three hundred miles from his position on the Arkansas.

In the next few years the French menace had increased steadily. Spanish traders brought to Santa Fe reports that *voyageurs* were advancing up the Red, the Canadian, and the Arkansas Rivers. At last, in 1719, Governor Val Verde had felt it necessary to go on a reconnaissance trip himself. He found no Frenchmen. Indeed, he had not traveled where he would have been likely to find them. If he had gone through Glorieta Pass and worked his way eastward across the plains [into northern Texas and Oklahoma], he would have learned something of value, for *voyageurs* were there. But instead, he had taken the old Raton Pass trail to El Cuartelejo. Perhaps his journey had been designed more for the purpose of demonstrating that he was taking a personal interest in matters under his jurisdiction than for the purpose of doing battle with intruders.

Whatever the case, he found out nothing that was not already known. In El Caurtelejo, Indians told him that French traders were on a large river to the north. It would soon be known as the South Platte, but Val Verde called it the Rio Jesus Maria. With nothing more than that to report, he turned his force of soldiers and Pueblos toward home.

He could have learned as much without leaving his office in Santa Fe. In fact, he did learn as much there shortly after his return, but it came in greatly embellished and far more alarming form. Not only were Frenchmen on the Platte, but they were also marching up it in forces six-thousand strong to invade New Mexico.

This report, of course, was false and most probably was a hoax perpetrated by some wise old Indian wag. But Val Verde was either gullible or as ignorant of geography as Pike would pretend to be. If, by some military miracle, the French had managed to send an army of six thousand men to take New Mexico without the offensive being discovered, they would hardly have sent it up the Platte, cut hundreds of miles southwest, and struggled through high mountain passes to reach Santa Fe. The trail up the Canadian River, which *voyageurs* long had been using, would have led them directly toward their goal over a much shorter and much easier route.

But Val Verde was taking no chances. By the following spring, 1720, he had a scouting party on the way north.

In command of this mission was Captain Pedro de Villasur. He had with him forty-three soldiers and sixty dependable Pueblo Indians. Foolishly, Villasur attempted to disguise his soldiers as Comanches by ordering them to let their hair grow long and to paint their faces. They deceived no one, least of all the Indians they met in El Cuartelejo.

Finding no Frenchmen on the Arkansas, the intrepid Villasur led his men on toward the north. They reached the South Platte early in August and went steadily on to the North Platte, which he called the Rio St. Laurent. Now his scouts brought him word that a large number of Indians were encamped near the confluence of the Platte branches.

Villasur forded the North Platte and turned down its

left bank. Four days later, he reached the junction and established his camp across the main river from a large Pawnee village. His overtures to arrange a friendly smoke with the Pawnees were coldly rejected. This unpromising situation caused him to move a short distance up the North Platte, recross the river to the slender tongue of land separating the two streams, and camp in what he considered a safer place.

At dawn on August 14, the Pawnees attacked with such suddenness and fury that Villasur was killed before he could arm himself. His men fought valiantly, taking a heavy toll of the Pawnees, but only nine soldiers and a few of the Pueblos lived to escape.

This early history was well known in St. Louis in the spring of 1806, and it entered significantly into the considerations of the Spanish agents. First, it meant that the country into which Pike allegedly was going was not unknown. It had been traversed and explored by Spanish *mercados* and French *voyageurs* for decades. Yet, Pike's mission assertedly was to discover the sources of its rivers, especially the sources of the Red River. But the sources had long been known, and the Red River, which the United States claimed was the southern boundary of Louisiana Territory, did not rise in the western mountains. It rose far east of them on the plains, far south of the Canadian River. Second, the nature of the climate of the country into which Pike was going was a matter of general knowledge from the Missouri River to Santa Fe. Its winters were long and bitter, and both mountains and plains were covered by impassable snows for long periods. Yet, Pike was scheduled to start for it in mid-July. He

[16]

could not possibly reach it before the frigid winds of fall had begun to blow down from the great peaks.

There seemed to be only one conclusion to be drawn. Pike did not intend to seek the source of any river. He intended to turn toward the south, into Spanish territory, while the weather was still good, as a spy for either the United States Army or General Wilkinson and Aaron Burr, and perhaps for both. Such a course would take him into warmer country before the onset of winter.

There was more evidence to support such a conviction. Pike would take with him only a score of men. Obviously this was an insufficient number if he had any thought of engaging Spanish forces in combat. But it was a contingent that could travel fast, observe Spanish defenses, and enter into negotiations with Indian leaders, and perhaps induce them to commit depredations against Spanish outposts and settlements. It would be a highly mobile force, unencumbered by heavy baggage, difficult to intercept, and even more difficult to overtake by troops traveling with a packtrain and the equipment required for extended operations in the mountains and plains.

The day on which the first dispatch about Pike started on its long journey from St. Louis to Chihuahua City, and the length of time consumed in delivering it to its destination, were details that some military clerk, in all likelihood, dutifully set down. If so, they too became buried beyond recovery in the mass of local records customarily given little care in the erroneous belief that they could be of no value to succeeding administrations. How significant these facts were in the dangerous game being played by Wilkinson, Burr, and Pike in 1806 would soon

[17]

be realized by harried and distressed executives of the American government.

The extent of Governor Salcedo's alarm was illustrated by the swiftness with which he took action. He must have received the first dispatch in May, perhaps as much as two months before Pike was scheduled to get underway. Within a few days, Salcedo had a detachment of at least a hundred regular cavalrymen riding hard for Santa Fe. The commander of this force, Lieutenant Don Facundo Melgares, carried orders that would permit him to quadruple its strength in New Mexico with mounted provincial militia and Indian interpreters and guides. Melgares and his men were to be fully supplied for an extensive reconnaissance of the plains and mountains bordering Spanish provinces on the north.

Preparations were carried out efficiently. In July, Melgares' small army, trailed by a packtrain of some two thousand animals, was descending the Canadian River, en route to the Great Bend of the Arkansas and the country of the Pawnees.

At the time, Pike and his little company had no more than left St. Louis.

Governor Salcedo's instructions to Melgares were simple and unequivocal. In essence, they were as follows:

1. Stop Pike.

2. Drive out or take prisoner every foreigner found on Spanish soil.

3. Negotiate treaties of peace and friendship with all wild peoples, and especially the Comanches, whom it was reported the Americans would approach in an attempt to secure them as allies.

Armed conflict was in the making in that summer of 1806, deep in the heart of the Great Plains, where Indian tribes had met in bloody encounters for countless centuries but where the warriors of civilized nations had never been engaged.

At stake was control of a vast part of the gigantic interior of North America.

2

It was in 1787 that Spanish officials in New Orleans had the misfortune to meet a young Kentucky merchant named James Wilkinson. They had no reason to suspect that behind him was a record that marked him as a leading artist of the doublecross and an avowed traitor to his country.

In that summer, Wilkinson had gone down the Mississippi with a fleet of flatboats heavily laden with cargoes of flour and tobacco. It was his hope, of course, to dispose of his products at a good profit, but what he wanted even more was an agreement with the Spanish that would allow American commodities from the interior (especially those from Kentucky) to be shipped through the port of New Orleans.

Spain had closed the Mississippi to American commerce, but Wilkinson, and some other businessmen with whom he was associated, had devised a plan they believed would meet with the approval of the Spanish King and result in the reopening of the river, at least to them. Their scheme was easier to plan than to accomplish, but Wilkinson refused to see in it any insurmountable barriers.

What Wilkinson proposed was the launching of an armed revolution in the region drained by the Ohio River and its tributaries to detach the western American settlements from the Union and establish a new republic under a commercial and military alliance with Spain.

Wilkinson was at the time only thirty years old, an indication of his natural acumen as a politician, his ability as a merchant, and his boldness as an adventurer. Yet, none of these fields had been the first to attract him.

At the age of seventeen, in Calvert County, Maryland, his birthplace, he had settled on a career as a physician. It was a profession for which he was totally unsuited. He was driven by an inherent and almost uncontrollable craving for the types of excitement and movement that a medical student could neither pursue nor afford. With the outbreak of the Revolutionary War, he quickly abandoned all thought of becoming a doctor and obtained a commission in the Continental Army.

Now Wilkinson found a use for what was unquestionably his greatest talent: intrigue. His capabilities in this shadowy realm were first recognized by another master of deceit, General Benedict Arnold, under whom he served in the Quebec Campaign.

And destiny, or perhaps the fates of war, contrived in this instance a situation unique in the history of the struggle of the colonies for freeom. With Arnold and Wilkinson was another officer who would win honors for intrepidity and daring. His name was Aaron Burr. Thus, the three men who would become America's most notorious traitors were brought together as staff colleagues on the field of battle.

A voluble, crafty extrovert, Wilkinson rose rapidly in rank. By 1777, he was an Adjutant-General. General Horatio Gates sent him to Philadelphia in 1778 to tell Congress about the American successes against the British commander, Burgoyne.

When it came to deceiving his own government, Gates did not permit either his oath of loyalty or his conscience to stand in the way. Ostensibly as a reward for what he termed brilliant actions, he recommended Wilkinson for a commission as a brigadier-general. The brilliant actions had been performed by other officers, but Wilkinson got the promotion.

There was a reason for Gates's deception: he needed Wilkinson. Both were involved in the Conway cabal, named for General Thomas Conway, an Irish soldier of fortune, who was also a participant. The cabal was designed to discredit General Washington, bring about his ouster, and make Gates Commander in Chief. In this cloudy affair, Wilkinson publicly unfurled his true colors for the first time. Hoping to make himself a hero and improve his own station, he informed on Gates and Conway.

The personal reaction of General Washington and the attitude of the Congress were not what Wilkinson had expected. Instead of being honored as a great patriot, he found himself in a precarious position, and he wisely resigned his commission before his own plotting became fully exposed.

The heat generated by the cabal quickly died away under the pressure of more urgent matters. At loose ends, Wilkinson decided it would be both safe and advantageous to reenter the Army. He found the door open to him. (Experienced officers were badly needed.) In 1779, he was appointed a general in the Quartermaster Corps.

(That was the year Zebulon Montgomery Pike, second child of Captain Zebulon and Isabella Pike, was born at Allamatuck, Somerset County, New Jersey. Fourteen years later, a reserved but strong-willed youth living at Fort Washington on the Ohio River [Cincinnati], Zebulon Montgomery Pike would begin his association with the deceptively attractive General, twenty-two years older than he, who would so greatly influence him for the rest of his life.)

The dull routine of the Quartermaster Corps did not satisfy Wilkinson's overwhelming propensity for action and adventure. Moreover, trouble was brewing over accounts that auditors were unable to bring into accord with known deliveries of supplies. In 1781, after two years in this quiet branch of the service, Wilkinson again resigned. Putting considerable distance between himself and the scene of his discrepancies seemed advisable, and he set out for the wilderness of the West.

Settling near the Falls of the Ohio, where the city of Louisville would rise, he was extraordinarily successful, prospering not only as a farmer and a merchant but quickly gaining prominence in the movement to make Kentucky a state.

Once again, Wilkinson was in his element as a dishonest politician. His schemes now were to secure commercial advantages, and although he pretended to cooperate with others who had the same ambition (and they were numerous), he was prepared to sell them out if necessary to obtain the money and influence he coveted.

It was with this idea dominating his thoughts that he went down the Mississippi in 1787 to New Orleans. His visions were grandiose. Like a panther stalking a deer, he quivered at the prospect of lapping the warm blood of a new kill.

The Eastern states, selfishly thinking of augmenting their own commercial interests and foreign trade, were willing to inflict economic strangulation on the Mississippi Valley by allowing Spain to keep the river closed to American traffic. If Wilkinson could secure Spain's aid in bringing about a rebellion that would separate the neglected territory from the United States, if he could fan the already smoldering fires of revolution into flame, he stood to win for himself unrestricted trading privileges. He could acquire vast land holdings, immense wealth, and great political power. Perhaps he might become head of a new republic and be hailed as the "Washington of the West."

Governor Esteban Miro of New Orleans was a gullible, if not altogether stupid, executive. He graciously received the charlatan from the North, swallowed his proposals, and pledged himself to make every effort to obtain approval of them by the King.

It would be an advantage, of course, if he could inform His Majesty that Wilkinson had become a Spanish subject. That was easily arranged. Wilkinson promptly swore allegiance to Spain. And Miro, delighted to picture himself as a builder of the Spanish colonial economy, readily granted Wilkinson the privilege of shipping

$30,000 worth of merchandise annually through the port of New Orleans.

Gloating privately over his success, Wilkinson went back to Kentucky. There he found that those smoldering fires of revolution had all but gone out. Kentuckians were resentful at the shabby treatment given them by Virginia and other Eastern states, but they were practical enough to realize that even if they succeeded in breaking away from the Union, they would have neither the numerical nor the financial strength to establish and support a new country. Also, they valued their freedom as Americans; most of them had fought and bled for it; and they were repelled by the thought of surrendering it to a monarch, thousands of miles away in Europe, who didn't know black strap from corn whiskey.

Disappointed but still determined to carry on with his treasonous scheme, Wilkinson went down the river again in 1789. There he received more bad news from Governor Miro. The Spanish King had flatly refused to enter into a conspiracy with the Americans. If the Kentucky merchants wished to enjoy the privilege of shipping through the port of New Orleans, they had two alternatives. They could pay a duty of fifteen percent, or they could move into Louisiana and become Spanish citizens, whereby they would not only escape the duty but also have a chance to obtain free land, enjoy religious tolerance, and have the right to sell tobacco through the King's monopoly on that product.

Understanding that he was temporarily blocked, Wilkinson refused to go home empty-handed. He talked the Spanish into paying him an annual salary of $2,000, as a reward for his efforts in their behalf, and offered to serve as a secret agent for them in the United States. There-after, in official Spanish correspondence, he was identified as "Number Thirteen."

At the time he became a Spanish spy, Wilkinson was engaged in scheming against the Spanish with the smuggler and notorious scoundrel, Philip Nolan, using Nolan to obtain information that he might furnish to anyone who would compensate him for it with favors or cash.

Nolan had been in San Antonio as early as 1785, posing as a trader but gathering military and political intelligence for sale. He would remain in close touch with Wilkinson in the ensuing years, and Wilkinson would send to Thomas Jefferson information, which he would call "specimens," that Nolan had gathered in Texas and Louisiana. Nolan would die under Spanish guns when he led a band of adventurers into the Brazos River country, assertedly to capture wild horses.

And it would be Zebulon Montgomery Pike who would make strenuous efforts to secure freedom for the survivors of the Nolan incursion, another link in the chain tying Pike to the schemes of Wilkinson.

After his return to Kentucky from New Orleans late in 1789, Wilkinson was in financial straits. He had spent his money too freely, and confident of success in his plan for a new republic, he had been careless of business and personal affairs.

But the astuteness of a great man, who was profoundly disturbed by the unrest and dissension in the Mississippi West and who was struggling to find solutions for the problems there, worked in Wilkinson's favor. George Washington concluded that the best way to achieve at last a temporary peacefulness on the western frontier was to remove the men who were advocating rebellion and disrupting the political unity of the nation, remove them not by punishment but by giving them something else to do.

That was President Washington's strategy when, in 1791, he appointed Wilkinson a lieutenant-colonel in the Army, and named several of Wilkinson's cohorts to civil and military posts.

3

WILKINSON WAS BACK in uniform, and he was still receiving some $2,000 a year as a secret agent for the Spanish. That was more than he got in his pay envelope as a lieutenant-colonel.

But he was a man destined to know good fortune while others about him, far more deserving and capable, suffered tragic reverses and death. He had been in service only a month, during which time he had seen some action in minor fights with Indians in the Ohio country, when the disastrous defeat of General Arthur St. Clair occurred near Greenville.

With the main body of his motley troops, and some two hundred of their wives and mistresses, St. Clair had been camped on the Wabash River. Half an hour before dawn on November 4, 1791, hundreds of Indians struck them in a surprise attack.

It was not a battle in which the Army could take pride. With the notable exceptions of St. Clair and a few experienced officers, the majority of the soldiers behaved like the shameless cowards they were. Many of them had been recruited from jails. Most of them were ignorant, shiftless, and degenerate, incapable of being inspired with any feeling of responsibility or loyalty. And all of them were badly clothed, badly fed, and badly paid.

Morally and mentally, the women who accompanied them were no better. Many of these unregenerate, profane, earthy females from the backwashes of civilization supplemented their meager existence by selling their filthy bodies. But cowardice was not one of their weaknesses. In the battle on the Wabash they fought like cornered cougars. And all but three of the more than two hundred perished.

Young Zebulon Montgomery Pike, then only twelve, would always know a glow of pride whenever he thought of the coolness and inordinate courage of his father, Captain Zebulon Pike, who took part in the debacle. He heard the story first from survivors, and later he read it in official reports.

Captain Pike's company, attached to the regiment commanded by General William Butler, had borne the brunt of the first Indian assault. Grievously wounded, General Butler had summoned Captain Pike to his side. "I can't live," he said. "Load my pistol and set me against that tree. You will tell my friends I died fighting."

Butler was shot and killed a few minutes later. The Indians who had seen him die admired his courage so greatly that they cut out his heart and ate it, hoping by this means to acquire some of the valor he had displayed.

Captain Pike was in command. He rallied his men, and coolly told them that their only chance of escape depended upon staying together and obeying his orders. After four hours of futile fighting, General St. Clair, realizing he was facing not a defeat but a massacre, ordered a general retreat. Somewhat miraculously, Captain Pike was able to lead his men in a successful withdrawal. It was unquestionably due to the tactic he employed. He instructed his men to load their weapons as they ran and to stop and shoot pursuing Indians only at his command.

After retreating in this manner for some two miles, he collapsed with leg cramps. His men went on, and he prepared to die fighting, as General Butler had done. But he was saved by an Army surgeon riding a horse and with a terrified boy clinging to him. "Don't just sit there and be butchered by these devils!" the surgeon shouted. "Take hold of the horse's mane." Pike obeyed, and was dragged to safety. The surgeon, the boy, and the Captain eventually rode the same horse to Fort Jefferson, thirty miles from the scene of the battle.

The Indians tortured the wounded to death, dancing and howling with delight at their screams. Some helpless prisoners were roasted at the stake. General St. Clair wrote to Secretary of War Dearborn: "They pulled out men's intestines bit by bit. They flayed others alive and slowly hacked or wrenched their limbs away. They dashed out the brains of children against the trunks of trees and flung their battered bodies into the brush. Some of the women were stretched naked upon the ground and run through with wooden stakes; others were cut in two after their breasts had been hacked away."

It was a catastrophe which shook the already insecure foundations of the young Federal government, making it cruelly apparent that militia from the gutters could not cope with Indians. From all parts of the country came cries for revenge. The settlements of the Northwest had to be protected, and it was the duty of the government to do the job. President Washington was equal to the crisis. He had known worse and more discouraging situations. General Anthony Wayne was given command of new regular Army forces authorized by a frightened Congress.

Lieutenant-Colonel James Wilkinson was promoted to the rank of brigadier-general. Seven months after returning to the Army, he was second in command to "Mad Anthony" Wayne.

In New Orleans, Governor Miro had been replaced by Hector, Baron de Carondelet, who, was if anything, a man of less ability than his predecessor. Within a year after taking office, Carondelet found himself facing a threatened invasion of New Orleans that was being organized by the French Minister in Washington, Citizen Edmond Genêt.

Although the invasion failed to materialize, Carondelet soon had new perils with which to deal. These involved fraudulent sales of lands by the Georgia Legislature to speculators. Carondelet feared that New Orleans was doomed, if not by a French-American invasion then by the intrusion of waves of settlers. He sought to bolster Spanish defenses and to form alliances with Indian tribes as he waited for the final blow to be struck.

Early in 1794, Carondelet received a lengthy report from Number Thirteen, Brigadier-General James Wilkinson of the American Army. It was a detailed account of the Genêt affair. Wilkinson took credit for preventing the invasion by the Genêt Legion of the Mississippi, as the movement was termed, and for saving New Orleans from falling into both French and American hands.

But that was not all Wilkinson did. He warned Carondelet that other offensives against New Orleans were in the making, and might well succeed, unless Spain engaged competent agents who could keep the frontiersmen peaceful while a separatist movement, which would bring the western areas under Spanish dominion, was being fomented and organized. Wilkinson, of course, was willing to serve—for suitable compensation—and would use his influence to recruit additional agents. Wilkinson had resurrected his old scheme. And he had a new pair of ears, a gullible new victim, to absorb it.

Desperate for assistance, Carondelet was delighted with Wilkinson's proposal. Obviously, he knew little of what had transpired between Wilkinson and Miro, and he did not take the trouble to find out. He wrote to Seville, pleading for the urgent dispatch of the necessary funds. But fearing they would not arrive before Wilkinson lost interest, he dipped into his own treasury. He gave Wilkinson $16,000.

There was much talk and bluster and activity by agents presumably enlisted by Wilkinson, but there was no revolution. By 1795, Carondelet realized that he had been duped.

Acting true to form, Wilkinson had not long been second in command in the West before he launched efforts to discredit and undermine General Wayne. He spread libelous stories against his superior and sought to arouse discontent and dissension among the troops from

Kentucky, who thought of him as one of their own. But he had little success, and he might have saved himself the trouble. In 1796, Wayne died.

Wilkinson became the commanding general of the American Army. He still retained his Spanish pension, and he had to do something to keep it from being cut off. At the time, efforts were being made to establish a southern boundary of United States territory east of the Mississippi. By stirring up both the Indian tribes and the Spanish with false information, Wilkinson was able to prevent a survey from being made for several months. It was not much, but it indicated to the Spanish that he was on the job.

Meanwhile, he kept in close communication with his old friend and fellow officer of the Revolution, Senator Aaron Burr, and in 1799 he visited Burr in New York.

Bigger and better schemes were in the wind.

4

THOMAS JEFFERSON LONG HAD BEEN interested in sending exploring expeditions across the continent. The acquisition of Louisiana made this legally possible and, in his view, mandatory. Yet, while preparing plans for the expedition which would be led by Lewis and Clark, the President had to give his attention to establishing a government for the new territory. He decided to appoint two commissioners to serve until Congress could get around to authorizing permanent legislative machinery. The logical candidates for the posts, it seemed to him, were two men who knew the West; and he named W. C. C. Claiborne, Governor of Mississippi, and General James Wilkinson.

Claiborne was neither enterprising nor very energetic. Rather, he was unimpressive and dull. Wilkinson's nature went to the other extreme. The General saw before him a new and unprecedented opportunity to sell his services to both sides, the Spanish and the American. And again he scurried down the Mississippi to New Orleans.

Wearing two impressive hats now—Commissioner of Louisiana and Commanding General of the Army—on this southern junket, he sold Spanish officials a record-breaking bill of goods. For the magnificent sum of $12,000, he turned over to them what he declared were confidential American plans for military operations in the Southwest. The plans were fraudulent.

At the same time, he dispatched to the War Department in Washington what was purported to be confidential intelligence on Spanish forces and defenses in the Southwest. They, too, were spurious.

In March, 1804, Congress divided Louisiana Territory into two parts. The area south of the 33d parallel would be known as the Territory of Orleans. The much larger part north of the parallel would be Louisiana Territory, more popularly called Upper Louisiana.

Wilkinson rushed to Washington. Claiborne could have the governorship of the Territory of Orleans. What he wanted was the governorship of the gigantic Louisiana Territory. With that portfolio in his pocket, he would be in a position to bill the Spanish for all they were worth. Besides, he would be the most powerful man in the West, with no end of chances to harvest a fortune, honestly or by other means.

Burr was President of the Senate, and although his political future looked unpromising, he was still powerful and influential. On May 23, 1804, Burr received a message from Wilkinson. It said: "To save time of which I need much and have little, I propose to take a bed with you this night, if it may be done without observation." He requested an immediate reply. If it was in the affirmative, he would appear surreptitiously at Burr's residence "at 30 after the 8th hour."

The shrewd and polished eastern politician, and the blustery and disreputable General from the West, in a secret meeting that spring night in Washington, began to refine plans for their treasonous conquests. Burr killed Alexander Hamilton in a duel less than two months later, ruining any hopes he may have held for ascension to higher political office.

Wilkinson got the appointment he sought, and he took office as Governor of Louisiana Territory in 1805.

Meanwhile, carrying out his part in his plot with Wilkinson, Burr attempted to extort money from the British and Spanish Ministers. The Spanish Minister promised Burr some funds, but all he could get from the British emissary was assurance that England would look with favor on any scheme to invade Spanish territory.

Sir Anthony Merry wrote London that Burr had informed him ". . . the inhabitants of Louisiana. [Territory] seemed determined to render themselves independent of the United States and that the execution of their designs is only delayed by the difficulty of obtaining previously an assurance of protection and assistance from some foreign power. . . ."

Burr, as well as Wilkinson, understood the falsity of such a statement. Both were fully aware that the events of the previous decade demonstrated that Americans of the states bordering the Mississippi and of Louisiana were not interested in a separatist movement.

Indicted for the murder of Hamilton in both New York and New Jersey, his political career ended, Burr set out for the West early in 1805 to confer with Wilkinson. They were scheduled to meet in Pittsburgh, but Wilkinson was not there when Burr arrived. With his daughter, Theodosia, and a small party of western politicians still friendly to him, Burr sailed down the Ohio in a private barge named the Ark. He was entertained in Lexington, Kentucky, by Henry Clay and in Nashville by Andrew Jackson.

It was June when Burr reached Fort Massac on the Ohio. Wilkinson was waiting for him. For four days, they held conferences in secret. Among the matters they discussed was the equipping of an army to invade Mexico.

And it was from Fort Massac at this time that Wilkinson wrote Lieutenant Zebulon Montgomery Pike to go to St. Louis and prepare with all speed for an expedition to explore the Upper Mississippi River.

Pike was then stationed at Kaskaskia. Excited and deeply thankful for the assignment, which would let him escape from the routine and monotony of small western posts, he started at once for St. Louis, which was not far away. With him he took his wife, Clarissa, their two small children, and a dozen infantrymen he knew to be reliable. Clarissa Pike would give birth to five children, but only one, a daughter, also named Clarissa, would long survive.

Pike knew that at the time Wilkinson was at Fort Massac to meet Burr. He was also aware of rumors and reports then circulating throughout the country that Burr was plotting to invade Spanish territory with a private army. And Pike had been too long in the confidence of Wilkinson not to understand that the General was not only sympathetic to Burr's scheme but harbored a similar one in which he, not Burr, would play the leading role.

Yet, Pike had no evidence to substantiate a suspicion that his assignment to the Upper Mississippi duty was in any manner related to the filibustering ambitions of either Burr or Wilkinson. And, of course, it was not. Not only was the direction wrong, but any event taking place in the frozen forests of northern Minnesota could hardly have had a bearing in those years upon events occurring in the plains and deserts of the Southwest.

Pike had good reasons to look upon the orders that came to him at Kaskaskia as part of the program to give reality to the dream of President Jefferson to obtain geographical and scientific knowledge of the West. At Wilkinsonville in 1801, and at Kaskaskia in 1803, Pike had met Meriwether Lewis. In the latter year, Lewis had been looking for suitable soldiers (but not officers) for the expedition to the Pacific which he and Clark would lead.

Pike would swear in later years that it was Lewis, not Wilkinson, who had first talked to him about exploring the Upper Mississippi. The assertion would be contained in an interrogatory in which he stoutly defended Wilkinson against charges of malfeasance and graft and absolved Wilkinson of all treasonous acts. "When Meriwether Lewis was at St. Louis, preparing for his expedition to the western ocean," Pike would testify, "he wrote me a letter, informing me it was the intention of the government of the United States, to detach several of the most enterprising officers on different routes, to explore our newly acquired territory of Louisiana, and inquired if it would be agreeable to me for him to recommend me for one of those commands; to which I answered in the affirmative. . . ."

The veracity of Pike's testimony in this instance would never be established. Neither Lewis's letter nor his alleged reply to it would be found. Nor would there be verification of his additional statement that he had "conceived" General Wilkinson's order to ascend the Mississippi "to be a continuance of the designs of the government, as suggested to me by governor Lewis."

Whether Pike was lying or telling the truth about the letters does not matter in this case. He did, indeed, have good reasons for his stand: he was covering his own involvement in Wilkinson's surreptitious fur trade activities; and he was concealing the true purpose of his northern journey, which was to bring pressure to bear, in the name of the United States Army, against Canadian fur trading companies that Wilkinson and his business associates wanted driven out of the northern areas.

He was being sent into a region which had been thoroughly explored over a period of a century by British, French, and American fur traders, a region in which trading posts had long been established: the immense area immediately west of the Great Lakes that would embrace the states of Wisconsin and Minnesota.

After assigning a barge and ten Army privates to escort Aaron Burr from Fort Massac to New Orleans, Wilkinson went directly back to St. Louis to counsel with Pike. There he directed preparations for not one but two small wilderness expeditions, both of which, he announced, would obtain geographical information, treat with Indian tribes, and locate suitable sites for military establishments. To the north would go Lieutenant Pike. To the west would go Lieutenant George Peter.

The reason for Peter's mission would be disclosed in Wilkinson's correspondence, and it would be clearly related to the Burr-Wilkinson plot to invade Mexico.

If Wilkinson himself would not disclose his design for sending Pike to the Upper Mississippi, it would, nevertheless, be revealed. As with the pieces of a jigsaw puzzle, when fragments of records and documents in official files were finally assembled and fitted together, an unmistakable picture evolved.

Lieutenants Pike and Peter had been gone from St. Louis more than a fortnight before Washington knew that Wilkinson had sent them out. It took at least three weeks for a letter from St. Louis to reach the Capital. The two expeditions had started early in August, 1805, but it was on July 27th that Wilkinson wrote the War Department: "I shall dispatch in a very few days two military exploring parties, the one for the Head of the Mississippi and the other for the Osage Towns—to ascertain the most commanding Sites for Military Posts and to obtain permission for their Establishment in the Spring early, also to ascertain the nature and extent of the Navigation, modes of Commerce, properties of the Soil, quality of water & Species of Timber, with whatever else may be deemed worthy of Note. . . ."

But also included in this same communication was the statement that ". . . to extend the name and influence of the United States to the remote Nations, will require considerable disbursements: and our relations to Spain and Britain on our Southern, Western & Northern unexplored frontiers Suggest the expediency of attaching to us, all the Nations . . . *Comanches,* who resort the tract of Country between the Osages and St. Afee, [Santa Fe] during the temperate Seasons, *merit particular attention,* because they constitute the most powerfull Nation of Savages on this Continent, *and have it in their power to facilitate or impede our march into Mexico,* should such movement ever become Necessary. It will be found difficult to draw this Nation to a conference, as they are perpetually at war with the Osages, yet with permission the attempt shall be made at Small expense *and I do not despair succeeding by next Spring. . . .*"

The italicized words throw light on the purpose of the trip of Lieutenant Peter. Wilkinson was using the machinery of the Army to prepare the way for his invasion of Mexico.

But his letter to Secretary Dearborn gave no clue to the real reason for his sending Pike to the wilderness of the Upper Mississippi; that he told only to Pike.

However, that exploration and discovery of the headwaters of the Mississippi were smoke screens was made clear in a single sentence of the orders Wilkinson handed to Pike on Juy 30, 1805: "You will proceed to ascend the main branch of the River, until you reach the source of it, *or the season may forbid your further progress, without endangering your return before the waters are frozen up.*"

It is superfluous to remark that the ultimate source of a river cannot be found simply by ascending its main branch.

Pike was to return to St. Louis *"before the waters are frozen up."* Yet, he did not start until August 9. To have reached a point near the source of the Mississippi before ice closed the northern rivers would have been impossible.

And as it happened, Pike and his men had gone only 100 miles above St. Anthony Falls [which are in Minneapolis] when cold, snow, and river ice trapped them, and they established a winter camp.

Wilkinson, of course, had understood that Pike could not get back to St. Louis before winter. But in writing to Secretary Dearborn on November 26, he complained that by continuing to seek the source of the Mississippi, Pike had "stretched his orders & we shall not hear of Him before the Spring."

In a report sent down river on September 23, Pike had been in the vicinity of St. Anthony Falls, and he had made it apparent that he had no intention of starting back.

In an earlier dispatch to Wilkinson, sent from Prairie de Chien, Pike had written about relations with Spain, and it revealed his familiarity with their inauspicious state. In the dispatch, he had proffered a "suggestion." It showed plainly that his thoughts were on matters which had nothing to do with the Upper Mississippi.

Three years later, when he was preparing his journals for publication, he would conclude that this suggestion put him in a bad light, as far as the public was concerned, and he would remove it from his manuscript and destroy it. At the time, he would be under suspicion of having participated with Wilkinson in treasonous activities.

But he was not a very good editor, even when it came to protecting himself. He failed to delete all evidence showing that the suggestion had been made. Remaining in the early September dispatch to Wilkinson, as it would be printed, was the statement: "The above suggestion would only be acceptable under the idea of our differences with Spain being compromised. . . .

"You see, my dear general, I write you like a person addressing a father: at the same time I hope you will consider me not only in a professional, but a personal view, one who holds you in the highest respect and esteem."

The only reference to the northern fur trade in Wilkinson's written orders to Pike appeared in the third paragraph: "It is interesting to our government to be informed of the Population and residence of the several Indian Nations, of the Quantity and Species of Skins and Furs they barter per annum, and their relative price to goods; of the Tracts of Country on which they generally make their hunts, and the People with whom they trade."

True, that would have been information enhancing the government's knowledge of the northern areas. But it would have been a great deal more valuable and meaningful to certain fur merchants of St. Louis, notably the Chouteaus and their confederate behind the scenes, James Wilkinson. For General Wilkinson had authority to issue fur trading licenses or to reject applications for them.

Pike knew what he was to do when he reached the Upper Mississippi, and he did it. As he advanced, he gathered all statistics he could regarding the fur trade. By the beginning of the year 1806, he deemed the material sufficient to let him carry out, with intelligence and without equivocation, the strong action Wilkinson had instructed him privately to take.

The Northwest Company, comprised almost entirely of British officials and factors, dominated the fur trade in the northern areas of United States territory. In February, from his camp at L'Aile du Corbeau, Pike sent a long letter to Hugh McGillis, a proprietor of the Northwest Company and director of its Fond du Lac Department, who was then at the company's Lake Leech post.

Coming from a person without diplomatic portfolio, who was traveling without sanction of the President, the State Department, or even the Secretary of War, the letter represented, undue assumption of authority, to say the least.

"As a member of the greatest commercial nation of the world," he told McGillis, "and a company long renowned for their extent of connections and greatness of views you cannot be ignorant of the rigor of the laws of the duties of imports of a foreign power.

"Mr. Jay's treaty, it is true, gave the right of trade with the savages to British subjects in the United States territories, but by no means exempted them from paying the duties, obtaining licenses, and subscribing unto all the rules and restrictions of our laws. [Jay's Treaty of 1794 with Great Britain was designed to settle difficulties which arose out of the Treaty of Paris and to regulate commerce, etc. Pike's reference to it showed he had given careful thought to his arguments, or that they had been prepared in advance for him.]

"I find your establishments at every suitable place . . . Our traders to the south . . . complain to our government, with justice, that the members of the N. W. company, encircle them on the frontiers . . . and trade with the savages on superior terms, to what they can afford, who pay the duties of their goods imported from Europe, and subscribe to the regulations prescribed by law.

[44]

"These representations have at length attracted the attention of our government. . . ."

Now Pike told McGillis that he had been "dispatched with discretionary orders" to investigate the situation, and that he had found the Northwest Company's "commerce and establishments, extending beyond our most exaggerated ideas, and in addition to the injury done our revenue, by the evasion of the duties, other acts which are more particularly injurious to the honor and dignity of our government."

The "other acts" were the "presenting of medals of his Britannic majesty, and flags of the said government, to the chiefs and warriors. . . ."

Pike delivered an unmistakable threat, advising McGillis that "strict justice would demand . . . total confiscation of your property, personal imprisonment and fines."

But Pike was prepared to be lenient, for "having discretionary instructions and no reason to think the above conduct was dictated through ill will or disrespect to our government . . . I am willing to sacrifice my prospect of private advantage, conscious that the government look not to interest, but its dignity in the transaction. . . ."

This generosity stated, Pike, thereupon, issued an ultimatum, to which he demanded the Northwest Company "strictly adhere." McGillis was to make representations to his agents "of the quantity of goods [merchandise to be used in trade with Indians] wanted the ensuing spring, for your establishments in the territory of the United States, in time sufficient, or as early as possible, for them to enter them at the C. H. [Custom House] of

Michilimackinac, and obtain a clearance and license to trade in due form." McGillis also was to "give immediate instruction to all your posts in said territory, under your direction, at no time and on no pretence whatever to hoist, or suffer to be hoisted, the English flag." And lastly, McGillis would "on no further occasion, present a flag or medal to an Indian: hold councils with them on political subjects, or others foreign from that of trade: but . . . refer them to the American agents, informing them that they are the only persons authorized to hold councils of a political nature with them."

Within a few days, McGillis had replied. His letter was diplomatic, conciliatory, and flattering. It had never been the intention of the Northwest Company to injure American traders. The presentation of British flags and medals of His Majesty to Indians would be halted. It was just an old custom, and they had "innocently and inoffen- sively" followed it to the present day. As for politics, the Northwest Company people were too ignorant "of the political views of nations" to discuss them, living as they did "in this rude and distant country." His company was in no way "averse to pay[ing] the common duties estab- lished by law," and would ever be ready to conform "to all rules and regulations of trade that may be established according to common justice."

McGillis revealed that he himself was no amateur diplomat, telling Pike that his "claim to honor, esteem, and respect, will ever be held in high estimation by myself and associates," and that the courage Pike had demon- strated in making his dangerous journey "will ever be preserved in the annals of the N. W. Company . . . we know we are in a country where hospitality and gratitude are to be considered above every other virtue . . . With great consideration and high respect for the government of the United States, allow me to express my esteem and regard for you."

It required more than an upstart lieutenant with twenty half-frozen men to intimidate the powerful Northwest Company. Moreover, McGillis was fully aware of the designs of St. Louis traders, to whom the acquisition of Louisiana Territory and the expedition of Lewis and Clark had opened a gateway to the North. The intrepid Northwesters, as they proudly called themselves, would play prominent parts in the northern fur trade until their company had been absorbed by the Hudson's Bay Company, and until the fur trading juggernaut of John Jacob Astor had moved up the northern rivers, more than a decade after Wilkinson's ultimatum had been issued by Pike.

Pike delivered major speeches to several Indian tribes on his Mississippi journey. They followed the same theme: denunciation of the British traders and an expression of the friendship and esteem of the Great White Father in Washington. But he did not forget to bring Wilkinson into the picture. Their Great Father, he told the Chippewas, had "directed his great war chief—general Wilkinson—at St. Louis, to send out a number of his young warriors . . . to make peace between them all. . . ."

General Wilkinson had told Pike: " . . . you may invite the great Chiefs . . . to pay me a visit." Pike did just that wherever he met with Indians in council. But none of them accompanied him back down the river. A few did wander into St. Louis at later dates, but not because of Wilkinson's invitation and not in the interest of negotiating an alliance of peace between the tribes; that desirable state would not exist until the Indians had been destroyed. They came largely to complain of being cheated, robbed, and murdered and to seek relief from the cruel treatment inflicted upon them by the American government.

Pike started on his Upper Mississippi venture on August 9, 1805, with one sergeant, two corporals, and seventeen privates, in a keel boat seventy feet long stocked with provisions for a journey of only four months. He got back to St. Louis on April 30, 1806, after an absence of eight months and twenty-two days.

If he had no personal interest in the fur trade, he did have a private motive, one for which he cannot be justifiably censored. He saw in the journey an opportunity to make a name for himself. He envisioned himself, as a result of it, under the Washington spotlight. It was an understandable dream of an ambitious young officer.

From almost every standpoint, the expedition was a failure. He drove no British trader from the North. He won no Indian allies for the United States. In scientific fields, he accomplished almost nothing. He discovered nothing. The lakes he identified as the source of the Mississippi were not that at all.

But he would receive a measure of the honor and fame he so eagerly wanted. In his annual message to Congress, delivered in December, 1806, President Jefferson would report on the results of the Lewis and Clark Expedition, and he would append the statement: "Very useful additions have also been made to our knowledge of the Mississippi by Lieutenant Pike, who ascended to its source and whose journal will be shortly made ready for communication to both Houses of Congress."

If Mr. Jefferson had not been accorded his unquestionable right to approve or disapprove of the Pike trip to the Upper Mississippi before it got underway, he would register no formal objection. General Wilkinson would not be reprimanded for exceeding his authority and neither would Pike.

But by the time Mr. Jefferson had got around to complimenting him, in December, 1806, Pike was struggling desperately to keep from freezing to death in the mountains beyond El Cuartelejo [Colorado], on his way to Spanish territory.

5

In his boyhood, Zebulon Montgomery Pike had known the hard life, the poverty, the brutalities, the barbarities, and the almost constant warfare of the trans-Allegheny country. His early homes were rocky woodland farms in Pennsylvania from which no more than a poor existence could be derived. His two brothers were afflicted with tuberculosis, although he and his sister, by some miracle, escaped the dread disease, which was so common among the western settlers at the time.

His father, Zebulon, had run away to sea as a young man. Returning to New Jersey at the outbreak of the Revolution, he had married, and then had joined the Continental Army. Zebulon Montgomery Pike's mother was Isabella Brown, the daughter of a farmer who distinguished himself as an officer in the war. Pike's middle name of Montgomery was given to him several years after his birth, in honor of General Richard Montgomery, who met death in the Quebec Campaign, and whom his father greatly admired.

Young Pike attended several country grade schools in Pennsylvania, but his education was frequently interrupted by family migrations and by economic vicissitudes. His mother sought to fill the gaps with her own teaching, and young Zebulon also received a good grounding in mathematics from a Mr. Wall (of whom nothing more is known), who considered him an intelligent and worthy pupil.

For several years after the Revolution, the elder Pike struggled to support his family as a farmer, but with little success. He was forty years of age when, in 1791, President Washington called for experienced military men to serve in a new campaign to subdue Indians of the Northwest Territories. Responding to the call, he received a captain's commission in the Pennsylvania militia, served under General St. Clair and then under General Wayne. In 1793, Captain Pike was commander of Fort Washington on the Ohio River. Like most of the officers, he had his family there with him.

Fort Washington was then the headquarters of General James Wilkinson, second in command to "Mad Anthony" Wayne.

As a boy only recently turned fourteen, Zebulon Montgomery Pike idolized Wilkinson. He saw him through the emotional eyes and the prejudiced, indestructibly loyal mind of youth as a military hero, a daring, dashing, gallant figure and an incomparable Indian fighter. It would be a conception, an image, that he would never be able to eradicate, in spite of all events which disproved it; and it would influence his own acts and thoughts—indeed, every aspect of his life—until the day of his death, at the age of thirty-four, on the battlefield of York in the War of 1812.

Zebulon Montgomery Pike knew only one ambition: to be a soldier; to emulate the two men he most revered (his father and Wilkinson); to rise to the rank of General of the Army of the United States; to know the fame and the adulation, and the comforts and the security and the prerogatives of that high office.

There could be no other career for him, and he launched himself upon it at the age of fifteen. In 1794, he was accepted as a cadet and was attached to his father's company. That he was strong enough, capable enough, and manly enough to be a regular soldier was soon apparent, and he was transferred to troops in the northern wilderness of Ohio. No record has been found of Pike's military actions during the next year. He claimed to have participated in the famous Battle of Fallen Timbers, but the claim has not been substantiated.

The Treaty of Greenville came in August, 1795. Under it, the Indians gave up the Ohio country and parts of Indiana. The war in this region was ended, and the way had been opened for western settlement. But Pike had no thought of leaving the Army.

As a noncommissioned officer [grade uncertain, but he was probably a sergeant], he had attracted the attention of General Wayne, and a month after the Greenville Treaty, he was given duties of considerable responsibility. In September, 1795, Wayne sent him to the far-western frontier, ordering: "You are to proceed with all possible dispatch for Fort Washington, from whence you will descend the Ohio . . . with barge and crew . . . who are to receive and obey your orders . . . and deliver the dispatches and stores committed to your charges to Captain Pike at Fort Massac . . . taking his receipt for same."

Young soldier Pike was back with his captain-father. Fort Massac was on the Ohio, only forty miles east of its junction with the Mississippi. Its chief function was to provide protection for settlers moving westward.

If the Indian danger in this area was minimal, a new danger had arisen to menace the migrations of Americans. For the first time, young Pike came up against the strained relations between the United States and Spain. The mouth of the great river had been closed by the Spanish, and His Catholic Majesty had left no doubt that he was determined to prevent infiltration of Americans into Spanish territories. Talk of American filibusters and invasions filled the air. To Fort Massac came orders to inspect all barges moving down the Ohio, and to stop the smugglers and filibusterers before they created open warfare with Spain.

Young Pike was busy transporting supplies and inspecting barges when, in 1796, his idol, Wilkinson, became commanding general of the Army. He not only saw Wilkinson, but carried out orders which came down from him.

Wilkinson, while occupied with his disloyal schemings and his work as a Spanish agent, had to give his attention to such routine matters as promotions and transfers, the shifting of frontier troops, and the building of new forts. One Pike, an heroic old soldier, was promoted to Major and transferred to Fort Pickering

[Memphis] in 1798. His military career was nearing its end. Another and much younger Pike, of whom Wilkinson was very much aware and whom he knew had demonstrated his abilities as a reliable soldier was still at Fort Massac.

On March 3, 1799, Zebulon Montgomery Pike received a commission as a second lieutenant. Eight months later, he was promoted to the rank of first lieutenant. It was apparent not only that he was in Wilkinson's favor but that Wilkinson had plans for him.

During his tours of duty at Fort Massac and at other stations along the Ohio River, the inherent qualities that distinguished Zebulon Montgomery Pike, both as a soldier and as a man, reached the high level of forcefulness they would not lose. Like his father and mother, both of whom were exemplary in their conduct and the standards by which they lived, he deplored the carousing and the imbibing and the sexual depravity that were inseparable ingredients of the frontier scene.

He was not a teetotaler, but he had no patience with men and women who drank to excess. If he ever engaged in an illicit affair, it was conducted in such secrecy that persons closest to him were unaware of it. Numerous of his contemporaries would write letters and biographical sketches of him after his death, but in none of them would there be a suggestion that he had ever enjoyed more than one romantic attachment. And that one involved the girl with whom he was in love and whom he married.

He was moral to a degree that many of his friends considered a fault, and he inclined at times to prudery and sanctimoniousness. He was given to lecturing the men under him about the evils of wenching and drink, and he arrested and punished those who ignored his warnings and made spectacles of themselves in public. But this he did no more, and perhaps not as much, for their welfare than for the reputation of his command.

Although Pike demanded discipline, and generally got it, his strictness was not extended beyond bounds to which he himself was not willing to adhere. It was not his way to inflict upon men of the ranks a duty or a peril he would not have shared with them, if necessary. He accepted the lot of his soldiers and the hardships of an assignment without complaint. Although he thought himself superior to the members of his commands (and, indeed, he was intellectually, morally, and physically superior to most of them), he made no public display of the attitude. With few exceptions, his men, especially those who made the wilderness journeys with him, not only respected him but sacrificed their bodies and their lives in unqualified loyalty to him.

These commendable qualities not only fitted him to lead and made him an outstanding young officer; they also made him extremely valuable and useful to a disreputable character like General Wilkinson.

Lieutenant Pike was not tall, standing four inches under six feet, but as a fellow officer would write of him, he was "tolerably square and robust . . . his complexion was ruddy, eyes blue, light hair and good features . . . very gentlemanly in his deportment, manner agreeable and polished, rather reserved in general . . . No officer could be more attentive, prompt and efficient . . . nor was there any more emulous to acquire a perfect knowledge of the military profession, nor more zealous, ardent and persevering in the pursuit of scientific improvement . . . he had acquired by his own persevering industry a tolerably good knowledge of the French language. . . ."

In his travels up and down the Ohio, Pike met the love of his life. She was his cousin, Clarissa Brown, the daughter of his maternal uncle, Captain James Brown. The Brown plantation, established shortly after the Revolutionary War, was near Sugar Grove, Kentucky, about fifteen miles below Cincinnati. It was a prosperous estate, with numerous slaves, and Captain Brown reputedly was worth more than $50,000, a veritable fortune in the year 1800.

Clarissa was eager to marry her handsome lieutenant cousin, but her father was less enthusiastic. The swain was poor, had no assured future, and his only income was his pay as a lieutenant. When Pike asked for Clarissa's hand, Captain Brown bluntly refused to sanction the union.

Pike quickly displayed the independence which was dominant in him. He persuaded Clarissa to elope. They fled to Cincinnati, were married, and established a home at Fort Washington.

General Wilkinson knew of Pike's marriage in defiance of his bride's father. He knew a good deal more about Pike than anyone, even Pike himself, realized.

During the first years of the century, Wilkinson frequently transferred Pike. He sent him to Washington with dispatches and assigned him to short tours at posts in Indiana and Illinois, to Fort Knox on the Wabash at

Vincennes, to Wilkinsonville, and at last, in 1805, to Kaskaskia. There Pike received the orders to go to St. Louis and prepare for the Upper Mississippi expedition.

The cards of the hand Pike would play had begun to fall into place, and Wilkinson was the dealer.

6

WITHIN THREE DAYS, and most probably sooner, after Pike and his weary company had returned to St. Louis from their northern expedition on April 30, 1806, he was told by General Wilkinson to make preparations for a journey to the Rocky Mountains.

The Wilkinson-Burr plans had been brought to completion during Pike's absence. A course of action had been formulated. The ultimate goal was an invasion of Mexico, but the successful execution of the necessary filibuster depended upon the occurrence of two major events: first, a complete breakdown of relations between Spain and the United States, and second, war between the two countries.

The situation looked promising. Claims and counter-claims over lands bordering the Gulf of Mexico, and the dispute over the boundaries of Louisiana Territory, had set the embers smouldering. Wilkinson, even more than Burr, was in a position to fan them into flames, and he did his best.

He sent the Spanish false reports about American plans of aggression, and he counseled them to hold and defend the Gulf Coast and to occupy the west bank of the Mississippi. An army of adventurers, he told Spain, was being formed to invade Mexico (his own scheme). He even advised the Spanish to arrest Lewis and Clark for intruding upon Spanish territory with a military company.

At the same time, he sent exaggerated and sometimes totally false dispatches to Secretary of War Dearborn and President Jefferson. These, he claimed, were based on Spanish intelligence reports on preparations to seize American lands and kill American settlers. He alarmed the War Department and the White House to such an extent that orders were issued to Indian Agents to cement friendly relations with western tribes and obtain assurances that they would fight on the American side in the event of war. Washington diplomatic notes to Spain contained thinly veiled warnings. Wilkinson feigned complete support for Mr. Jefferson's program to gain useful scientific and geographical knowledge through western expeditions. He fed unfounded information to newspapers which resulted in inflamatory articles on criminal Spanish conspiracies to kill Americans and confiscate American goods.

To Secretary Dearborn in September, 1805, Wilkinson wrote with deceptive smoothness: "I recollect having once disagreed with you, as to the Practicability of carrying an expedition from this point [St. Louis] into New Mexico, and my objections were founded on the length of the March, and the difficulty of Subsisting the Troops—

but these obstacles have vanished . . . I find that we may derive abundant supplies of meat from the fields and Forests, through which the route takes its direction, and that the practicable distance does not exceed 900 miles, over a surface in general Smooth, with the intervention of one mountain only. . . .

"Should We be involved in a War, (which Heaven avert) and it should be judged expedient to take possession of New Mexico, magazines of flour, ammunition and arms, particularly Cavalry equipment with ten field Pieces, should be dispatched up the Arkansas or Osage River about the 1st of March, and a Corps of 100 Artillerists, 400 Cavalry, 400 Riflemen and 1100 Musquetry, should move from this place about the 20th of April. . . ."

Wilkinson was fully cognizant of the political, social, and religious powers of the Catholic Church in the Spanish provinces, and he advised Dearborn that the "judicious and rapid" movement of the invasion troops should be "attended by the Cross for your Banner, and a band of Irish priests who have been educated in Spain—of whom I know a dozen. . . ." With this ecclesiastical support, he believed that the United States would "take possession of the Northern Provinces without opposition. . . ."

Wilkinson continued to pound away on the subject, writing Dearborn on November 26, 1805: " . . . I most ardently implore that we may not be forced to War, because I seek repose & we are not indeed prepared for it, that is against European troops—yet if we must draw the sword, the whole of the troops destined to operate West of the Mississippi should be mounted, whether Gun-men or sword-men, because every Man of the Enemy will be found on Horse Back, and the composition should be such as I have described in a former Letter—If anything should be done from this Quarter direct, and I might be indulged to recommend my officers, to plan & Lead the expedition, If I do not reduce New Mexico, at least, in one Campaign, I will forfeit my Head."

In one reply, Secretary Dearborn declared: "I am more fully convinced by your communication, of the practicability, if necessary, of a military movement, either by the Platt, the Osage or the Arkansas, to the Eastern part of Mexico . . . and I am not sure that a project of that kind may not become necessary. . . ."

It would have been very helpful to Wilkinson if he could be in command of a force of the kind he proposed, en route to take possession of Mexico. He must have smiled with satisfaction at the gullibility and trustfulness of Dearborn.

The contemplated action had not been sanctioned by the time Pike got back from the North, but Wilkinson, never a man to delay unnecessarily, was ready to proceed along another tangent.

Pike, however, was not as blind to realities in the West as was the Secretary of War, two thousand miles away in Washington. If Pike was susceptible to flattery, if he was ambitious for fame and promotion, if his admiration of Wilkinson was indestructible, he was practical enough and intelligent enough to recognize the implications and the dangers of his assignment to take a company to the mountains. Moreover, he was, although only twenty-seven, a veteran soldier of the frontier. He knew war. He knew Indians. Even more important, as far as

Wilkinson was concerned, was his knowledge and understanding of both the economics of the West and the tense, brooding problems in the deteriorating Spanish-American relations.

Wilkinson understood the situation. He had sent Pike to the Upper Mississippi, but that was territory indisputably owned by the United States. He knew that he could not hope to send Pike off into Spanish territory merely on the pretext of finding the headwaters of some river. For Wilkinson knew that Pike would be suspicious, that Pike would quickly reach the conclusion that he was a pawn in some scheme that might well be detrimental to the best interests of the United States.

The problem Wilkinson had to resolve to his own satisfaction was not whether he should take Pike into his confidence, but how much he should tell him. He realized very well that he could never persuade Pike to commit any act that might be interpreted as disloyal to the Army or to the country. Pike's pride in the uniform and his patriotism were inflexible.

Wilkinson found the answer he wanted, and he was convinced that it would be both advantageous to him while disturbing Pike's conscience not at all. Spying was neither disloyal nor could it be conceived in any manner as treasonous. Spying was a legitimate military operation. Not only would Pike think of it in that way, but he would willingly accept orders in such a guise—without question. A little sugar in the form of a promise of promotion would serve to increase Pike's enthusiasm for the project. And it would not be difficult to secure approval of a captaincy for him. Of course, if Pike's spying resulted in his death at the hands of the Spanish, that would be regrettable, but it must be thought of as one of the hazards of the game.

Wilkinson was right. Pike was willing to act in the spying role. His success could bring him nothing but honors, and the prospect of gaining a captaincy in the near future greatly cheered him. He worked feverishly to prepare his journal of the Upper Mississippi expedition for submission to the President and the Congress. The only dampers on his enthusiasm were his need of money and the frail condition of Clarissa. He feared she might not have long to live, and he despaired of having to leave her. Yet, he saw no alternative. Resigning from the Army would place him in an even more precarious financial condition. His father-in-law had not forgiven him, and there was no assurance that money would come from that quarter, even in a time of dire need. He was unfitted to pursue any other career. Besides, resignation would mean the sacrifice of years of struggle to rise, not to mention the fame he felt was almost within his grasp.

He would go West, praying that Clarissa's health would improve and that she would live to share the limelight, emoluments, and privileges of the high rank and distinction he was convinced he would receive.

Wilkinson, meanwhile, was not giving all his attention to military matters and political graft, or to the sending out of spies. St. Louis was booming, bathed in a rosy glow of prospective economic opportunities that were reflected from the signatures on the document that made Louisiana Territory a part of the United States. In the three years which had passed since the acquisition, every way of life there had been drastically transformed. As greedy as he was crafty and dishonest, Wilkinson was taking steps he believed would bring him riches never to be acquired as a military man or as a civil governor, or even under the combined offices. But holding these offices did open doors that otherwise might have been closed to him.

7

It had been well within the memory of the living, the spring of 1764, that the noise of hammering and sawing first broke the wilderness silence on a benchland above the Mississippi River, just a short distance below the mouth of the Missouri.

Pierre Laclede Liguest and thirty men, nearly all of whom were craftsmen, were building the settlement they had named St. Louis in honor of the patron saint of their King.

Maxent, Laclede, and Company had been given a grant for the exclusive trade of the Missouri and Upper Mississippi Rivers, but in the time it had taken Laclede and his men to travel by keelboat upstream from New Orleans and start the settlement, the grant had been made legally worthless by the transfer of Louisiana from France to Spain.

In Laclede's small company was a young man of

fourteen, Auguste Chouteau. Despite his youth, Laclede considered Chouteau an able and trustworthy assistant, and he gave him the duty of overseeing the construction work. Trading with the Indians was soon begun, and Chouteau took an active part in it. This was the beginning of the fur trading dynasty he would found, which for more than a century would be influential in the economic development of the West.

The ceding of Louisiana to Spain brought no major changes to the fur trade. French traders had little difficulty operating under most of the governors who came and went during four decades, a situation rare, if it were to be found at all, in the annals of Spanish colonies of the Western Hemisphere.

The original traders formed partnerships and reached agreements which created spheres of operation among the many Indian tribes. In the main, they respected the claims of each other. Even though their numbers increased and competition developed, expansion was always possible and trade routes were pushed steadily farther into the wilderness.

Families and relatives were brought from New Orleans, even from the West Indies and from Europe, and with them came the culture and the manner of living which they had known in their homelands. Some spacious residences rose among wide gardens and grounds shaded by great trees. Slaves polished carriages, groomed good horses, shined metal doorplates, kept log fires burning in handsomely furnished rooms, and silver flatware caught the light of candles on dinner tables covered with imported linens.

This good taste, affluence, and prosperity, however,

were to be enjoyed in only a few places in St. Louis. Its tawdriness increased commensurately with its growth, and by 1800, it presented in the larger part a ragged cluster of clapboard, stone, log, and earthen buildings, a conglomeration of shacks, hovels, cabins, dilapidated shops, and warehouses edging the graceful, well-tended residences of the wealthy fur merchants.

Up to this time, neither the dominant Chouteau clan, *père et fils,* nor other prominent traders (among them the dynamic and shrewd Spaniard, Manuel Lisa) had displayed more than a casual interest in the far northern country of the Upper Missouri. They had left it mostly to the British, being satisfied with conditions and the amount of trade obtainable much nearer home. They had always made good money among the tribes of the Lower Missouri, the Illinois, and even as far south as the Arkansas and westward a considerable distance on both the Kansas and the Platte.

The people of St. Louis and other towns of Upper Louisiana, being predominantly of French origin, were delighted, of course, when the great territory was returned to France. But they did not share the extreme ideas of the motherland revolutionists. They preferred the quieter, easier ways of their forefathers. Political innovations and modern social theories had no attraction for them. In dealings among themselves, they were honest and punctilious, so that they had little need of courts or lawyers. Dealings with Indians were, however, another matter. Trading was trading, and the sharpest deserved the most benefits. They were cruel and unsympathetic with the people from whom they derived, and upon whom they depended for, their living.

Suddenly, seemingly almost overnight, everything St. Louis had known for so long was changed. Louisiana was sold to the United States. Old residents wept as the standard of the French Republique was supplanted by the Stars and Stripes. But, like it or not, they were Americans.

This fact was quickly made apparent to them in ungentle ways. Across the Mississippi poured a heterogeneous parade, accompanied by a lasting uproar. American traders, merchants, hunters from Virginia, Kentucky, and Tennessee, river louts, prostitutes, soldiers, government officials, gamblers, thieves, degenerates, and false prophets crowded the streets and the river front. As if by magic, brothels, saloons, cafes, shops and inns appeared and all manner of ramshackle establishments as well, some of them no more than holes dug in the bank of the river.

The Upper Missouri and other northern rivers were American territory, and they ran through a land rich in furs. There was nothing to prevent newcomers from going into it, nor was there anything to stop them from intruding in the areas which old St. Louis trading families, especially the Chouteaus, had for more than two generations considered their exclusive domains.

There was nothing, that is, except the man who was both commanding general of the American forces and Governor of the territory. And Auguste Chouteau, still head of his clan, understood that. But Auguste Chouteau, true to his independent character, tried to handle things himself before joining ranks with Wilkinson. He went to Washington and had an audience with President Jefferson.

Boldly Chouteau asked that he be given the right to issue all licenses to trade with Indians, and that meant also the right to reject applications for them, and the "direction and all the profits of the trade carried on by the government with all the Indians of Louisiana." For this privilege he would replace all capital expended by the government in the Indian trade. Mr. Jefferson refused him.

In a counteroffer, Chouteau lowered his sights. He asked for "exclusive trade with the Osages, to be effected by granting licenses only to his agents." Mr. Jefferson did not refuse him. Fearful of antagonizing the influential St. Louisan, whom he thought "may be either useful or dangerous," the President asked Chouteau to put his request in a letter to Secretary of War Dearborn.

Chouteau did not get all he wanted in Washington, but he did secure licenses which put him in a powerful position in the Indian trade.

Wilkinson studied the situation with great interest. His conclusion was that a private alliance with the Chouteaus would be greatly to his own advantage, and he effected it. This put Wilkinson in the fur trade, not only with the Osages but with several other tribes on the Missouri and Mississippi in whose homelands the Chouteaus had licenses to trade.

The Chouteaus were agreeable because Wilkinson had something to offer in return. Indian affairs came under the jurisdiction of the War Department, and as ex officio Indian Agent of Louisiana, Wilkinson had the authority to issue licenses for the Indian trade. He rejected applications of traders proposing to operate in competition with the Chouteaus. He issued a proclamation forbidding British traders from entering Louisiana Territory, and this edict had a sound legal basis. Jay's Treaty had allowed

Canadians certain trading privileges in the Old Northwest of the United States, but said nothing about extending these privileges to any territory the United States subsequently acquired. Pike had mentioned this point in his letter to Hugh McGillis of the Northwest Company, another indication that he was not only well informed on the subject but understood the trend of Wilkinson's thinking. Strict enforcement of Wilkinson's proclamation would have the effect of channeling the fur trade of the northern rivers into the hands of the Chouteaus.

As he had done in the case of Pike's Upper Mississippi trip, Wilkinson would give Pike unwritten orders having to do with the fur trade of the regions, including New Mexico, through which the Lieutenant [or Captain] was to pass on the western expedition. And in complying with them, Pike would make frequent mention of the trading activities he observed, speak on the future possibilities of the trade in the Southwest, and note that furs were transported from New Mexico to Chihuahua and other places in Mexico.

But things were not to work out in St. Louis as Wilkinson had expected. He would not reap the immense rewards he had anticipated from the fur trade. That, however, would not be because he did not try. It would be because complaints to Washington about his corruption and stealing would bring his removal as Governor. And it would be because the exigencies of the troubles with Spain would cause him to be sent down the Mississippi. He would not return to St. Louis after 1806, but he would continue as the commander of the American military forces in actions against the Spanish in eastern Texas.

8

WILKINSON HAD CONTRIVED SEVERAL reasons to justify Pike's western expedition, but the turn of affairs played into his hands in a way that would have made a part of the journey mandatory even if he had had no other excuse for it.

Fifty-one Osage men, women, and children who had been captured by the Potawatomis had been ransomed by the United States, and the Indian Department had ordered that they be returned to their homes. President Jefferson himself had been highly exercised by the situation, and had written Governor William Henry Harrison of Indiana Territory: "The late stroke of the Poutewatamies on the Osages must be strongly reprimanded, and no exertion spared to recover & restore the prisoners & make satisfaction for the killed. The Indians on this side of the Mississippi must understand that the river is now ours, & is not to be a river of blood."

In addition to these survivors, a deputation of eight Indian leaders—an Oto, two Pawnees, and five Osages—who had reached St. Louis from a visit to the Great White Chief in Washington, were to be escorted to the Osage villages on the Osage River. Their protection was of paramount importance to good relations between their peoples and the United States. No chances were to be taken that they might suffer injury en route to their destination.

Wilkinson seized upon these matters in thoughtfully preparing the written orders for Pike. Given to Pike on June 24, 1806, these orders said:

"Sir,

"You are to proceed without delay to the Cantonment on the Missouri, [a short distance north of St. Louis at Belle Fontaine] where you are to embark the late Osage captives and the deputation recently returned from Washington, with their presents and baggage, and are to transport the whole up the Missouri and Osage rivers to the town of the Grand Osage.

"The safe delivery of this charge at the point of destination *constitutes the primary object of your expedition;* therefore you are to move with such caution as may prevent surprise from any hostile band, and are to repel with your utmost force any outrage which maybe attempted.

"Having safely deposited your passengers and their property, you are to turn your attention to the accomplishment of a permanent peace between the Kansas and Osage nations; for which purpose you must effect a meeting between the head chiefs of those nations, and are to employ such arguments, deduced from their own obvious interests, as well as the inclinations, desires, and commands of the president of the United States, as may facilitate your purpose and accomplish the end.

"A third object of considerable magnitude will then claim your consideration. It is to effect an interview and establish a good understanding with the Yanctons, Tetaus, or Camanches.

"For this purpose you must interest White Hair, of the Grand Osage, with whom and a suitable deputation you will visit the Panis [Pawnees] republic, where you may find interpreters, and inform yourself of the most feasible plan to bring the Camanches to a conference. Should you succeed in this attempt—and no pains must be spared to effect it—you will endeavor to make peace between that distant powerful nation and the nations which inhabit the country between us and them, particularly the Osage; finally, you will endeavor to induce eight or ten of their distinguished chiefs to make a visit to the seat of government next September, and you may attach to this deputation four or five Panis and the same number of Kansas chiefs.

"As your interview with the Camanches *will probably lead you to the head branches of the Arkansas and Red Rivers, you may find yourself approximated to the settlements of New Mexico. There it will be necessary you should move with great circumspection, to keep clear of any hunting or reconnoitering parties from that province, and to prevent alarm or offense; because the affairs of Spain and the United States appear to be on the point of amicable adjustment,* and moreover it is the desire of the president to cultivate the friendship and harmonious intercourse of all the nations of the earth, particularly our near neighbors the Spaniards.

"In the course of your tour, you are to remark particularly upon the geographical structure, the natural history, and population of the country through which you may pass, taking particular care to collect and preserve specimens of everything curious in the mineral or botanical worlds, which can be preserved and are portable. Let your courses be regulated by your compass, and your distances by your watch, to be noted in a field-book; and I would advise you, when circumstances permit, *to protract and lay down in a separate book the march of the day at every evening's halt.*

"The instruments which I have furnished you will enable you to ascertain the variation of the magnetic needle and the latitude with exactitude; and at every remarkable point I wish you to employ your telescope in observing the eclipses of Jupiter's satellites, having previously regulated and adjusted your watch by your quadrant, taking care to note with great nicety the periods of immersions and emersions of the eclipsed satellites. These observations may enable us, after your return, by application to the appropriate tables, which I cannot now furnish you, to ascertain the longitude.

"*It is an object of much interest with the executive to ascertain the direction, extent, and navigation of the Arkansas and Red Rivers;* as far, therefore, as may be compatible with these instructions and practicable to the means you may command, I wish you to carry your views to those subjects; and should circumstances conspire to favor the enterprise, that you may detach a party with a few Osage to descend the Arkansas under the orders of

Lieutenant Wilkinson,* or Sergeant Ballinger, properly instructed and equipped to take the courses and distances, to remark on the soil, timber, etc., and to note the tributary streams. This party will, after reaching our post on the Arkansas, descend to Fort Adams [on the Mississippi] and there await further orders; and you yourself may descend the Red River, accompanied by a party of the most respectable Camanches, to the post at Natchitoches, and there receive further orders.

"To disburse your necessary expenses and to aid your negotiations, you are herewith furnished *six hundred dollars'* worth of goods, for the appropriation of which you are to render a strict account, vouched by documents to be attested by one of your party.

"Wishing you a safe and successful expedition, I am Sir with much respect and esteem your obt. sert."

There was nothing in the orders to which the Secretary of War might object, if he ever saw a copy of them. Making scientific and geographical observations met with official administration policy, as did negotiating treaties of peace with Indian tribes.

Yet, it would not have taken a thoughtful student of the document long to understand that it said much more than a quick reading of it would indicate. As for Pike, in close consultation with Wilkinson, he need not have read his orders at all to know what the primary object of his trip was: to observe and report to Wilkinson on a feasible route to New Mexico which might be followed by an invading force.

Before receiving his initial orders, Pike had been

* James B. Wilkinson, the General's son, who would be a member of the expedition.

informed by Wilkinson that he would be accompanied, at least on part of the journey, by the General's son and Ballinger and that he would confer with the Osage leader, White Hair. He did not need to have an explanation from Wilkinson for the assignments.

In 1806, two years before he became a captain, Lieutenant James Biddle Wilkinson was in his early twenties and had been in the Army five years, for most of that period on his father's staff. Under other circumstances he would not have been able to meet the strenuous demands and hardships of frontier military life, for since boyhood, his health had been on the frail side, and he was at times highly nervous. This precarious physical condition had evoked genuine sympathy in the General, but while his first consideration was to protect his son, it was supplemented by other reasons for keeping him under his wing. Lieutenant Wilkinson was highly intelligent, thorough in the performance of his duties, displayed no lack of personal courage, and manifested an unqualified loyalty to his commander-father. Both his capabilities and his characteristics made him a valuable and trustworthy aide.

Sergeant Joseph Ballinger stood in an entirely different category. He was a tough, uncouth, uneducated frontiersman, and he had first participated in the nefarious actions of Wilkinson in 1789. At that time, he had been used as a messenger between Wilkinson and Spanish officials, delivering the false information Wilkinson prepared for his foreign employers and bringing Wilkinson the pay he received as a Spanish agent. For sixteen years thereafter, Ballinger had served Wilkinson faithfully in undercover work.

Pike participated in falsifying Ballinger's military records. Told by Wilkinson to take Ballinger West with him, Pike enlisted Ballinger in St. Louis early in 1806 for five years. Ballinger was paid an enlistment bounty of $12, and was immediately promoted to sergeant.

Later, on the muster roll of his western expedition, prepared in 1807, Pike would record the date of Ballinger's enlistment as 1802. This made the sergeant eligible for discharge, after allegedly serving five years. And Pike gave it to him.

As for the Osage, White Hair, Pike was aware that his position as a tribal leader was largely, if not entirely, due to the support given him by the Chouteaus. White Hair was not in fact the great Osage chief the Chouteaus made him out to be in their dealings with the War Department and the Indian Bureau. He was a paid confederate of the Chouteaus, working among Plains Indians in their interests. In view of the alliance Wilkinson had with the Chouteaus, White Hair's activities were of no little concern to the general.

Pike made no objection to performing this extracurricular service for the man he had so long revered.

9

HANDICAPPED BY A LACK of training in scientific fields, Pike was not above resorting to a bit of plagiarism. As he worked on reports of his Upper Mississippi venture, he had access to statistical data on Indians east of the Missouri River which had been gathered by Lewis and Clark and had been sent down the river to St. Louis by them early in 1805. Pike prepared a chart on the subject that was astonishingly similar to one submitted by William Clark.

On July 2, 1806, Pike completed his "reports, observations, and journals" of the Mississippi voyage, and in a letter to Wilkinson on that date, he revealed his familiarity with the Lewis and Clark material by the remark that "I differ materially from capt. Lewis, in my acount of the numbers, manners, and morals of the Sioux."

Pike had been forced to rush his rewriting and editing. Dissatisfied with his work, he took occasion to remind Wilkinson that he had "scarcely returned to St. Louis, before the voyage now in contemplation [to New Mexico] was proposed to me, and after some consideration, my duty—and inclination in some respects—induced me to undertake it. The preparations for my new voyage prevented the possibility of my paying that attention to the correction of my errors, that I should otherwise have done." And he expressed the hope that his statement would "be deemed a sufficient apology for the numerous errors, tautologies and egotisms which will appear."

Wilkinson could not have cared less than he did about the content and condition of Pike's manuscripts. He had far more urgent matters to consider. And not the least of them had to do with the necessity of supplementing the orders he had given Pike on June 24.

On July 12, he commanded Pike to leave for the West on the following day. He was especially worried about the way Pike would get along with White Hair and other Indian politicians, and he sent Pike copies of "talks" which were to be made to White Hair and to Makes-Tracks-Going-Away, the chief of a splinter band of Osages dwelling on the Verdigris River. They had been induced to separate from their people in 1802 by Pierre Chouteau, a son of Auguste, who controlled the trade with them.

Now, Wilkinson obviously thought it best to include in the same letter of July 12 to Pike a phase of the western expedition which had not been previously disclosed in any official communications. He wrote: "Doctor Robinson will accompany you as a volunteer. He will be furnished medicines, and for the accommodations which you give him, he is bound to attend your sick."

This was not news, however, either to Pike or to Dr. John Hamilton Robinson. It was merely confirmation of an understanding reached some weeks earlier.

Dr. Robinson, a Virginian only twenty-four years of age, had been practicing surgery and medicine in St. Louis little more than a year. He had become a close friend of Wilkinson, and the General had sought a commission for him in the Army, with the intention of stationing him at Cantonment Belle Fontaine, where a physician was badly needed. By the summer of 1806, however, the appointment had not been approved by the War Department.

In the meantime, Wilkinson had developed other plans for Robinson. Pike was fully aware of them. He did not altogether approve, but he kept his counsel dutifully, having no desire to antagonize the General over an arrangement that already had been completed and that he knew the General would not change.

The agreement Wilkinson had made with Dr. Robinson involved more than his professional services on the western expedition. Handsome, intelligent, with polished manners, Dr. Robinson also displayed a suavity and a talent for diplomacy that were not expected, and were seldom evidenced, in a man of his years. Wilkinson not only shrewdly appraised these qualities but gave thought to capitalizing on them to his own advantage. Experience had taught him their value in dealing with emissaries of a foreign government.

He persuaded Dr. Robinson to accompany the Pike company as a spy against the Spanish. And Pike would contribute thought and effort to making Dr. Robinson's mission successful.

Wilkinson's cleverness was demonstrated by his

adoption of a device that he believed might be useful to Dr. Robinson as an espionage agent. For some time, fur traders and merchants of St. Louis had sought means of establishing trade relations with Santa Fe, which they thought would open the commercial gate not only to southwestern Spanish regions but also to Mexico. For some years, traders had pushed far out the Platte, the Kansas, the Arkansas, and other plains rivers. When the French owned Louisiana Territory, the reticence of the Spanish to permit traders to enter Santa Fe was understandable. When the province belonged to Spain, however, there was no good political reason why trade should not have been conducted with the New Mexico capital. But it did not develop because the Spanish could not overcome their deeply ingrained distrust and suspicion of either French or British traders. When Louisiana became American territory, the same feelings not only endured but became intensified.

But the hope of tapping the lucrative southwestern market persisted in the St. Louis traders. In 1804, William Morrison, a leading merchant, made an attempt to penetrate the Spanish barrier. He sent an experienced French Creole trader, Baptiste La Lande, to make his way to Santa Fe with a modest assortment of trade goods.

La Lande set a course for the Pawnee Villages [on the Republican River near the Kansas-Nebraska border], cut northwestward to the Platte, and followed the South Platte toward the Rocky Mountains. With him from the Pawnee villages, which he previously had visited, went a group of his Indian friends. They followed trails over which intertribal Indian traders had passed for centuries. Somewhere along the South Platte, they turned south to the Arkansas, which La Lande thought Americans considered the northern boundary of Spanish territory.

A daring but cautious man, La Lande sent several of his Indian companions to Santa Fe to find out if he would be permitted to proceed, and settled down in a camp to await their return. When they did return, several days later, they were accompanied by a contingent of soldiers. La Lande was welcome to enter Santa Fe, and the soldiers had been sent to escort him there. This was a polite way of saying that La Lande would be taken to Santa Fe.

Spanish officials had no objections to his selling his goods, and he disposed of them at high prices. Thereupon came a *suggestion* from Governor Joaquin del Real Alencaster that La Lande might enjoy spending some time in the pleasant environment of Santa Fe. To make La Lande's stay all the more pleasant, certain privileges would be granted to him; and should he choose to establish his residence there, he would be given a piece of land.

Behind the facade of this courtesy was Governor Alencaster's fear—belated, to be sure—that in permitting La Lande to return to St. Louis, he would be establishing a precedent that would prove dangerous to his own political career. Orders from Chihuahua had made it clear that all foreign traders were to be kept out of New Mexico.

If La Lande understood the nature of his predicament (and there seems little doubt that he did), he found the inducements offered to him difficult to reject. St. Louis was far away, in another world. Life was, indeed, pleasant and full in Santa Fe, and especially enticing were the attractive *senoritas* made available to him. He pocketed Morrison's money, established a home, and settled down with the bedmate, or bedmates, he found most satisfactory.

In St. Louis, after waiting anxiously for word from La Lande for two years, Morrison talked to Wilkinson about the matter. Absconding with trade goods was a major crime, but Wilkinson was less interested in seeing justice done than he was in using the situation to his own advantage.

He proposed that Morrison place his claim against La Lande in Pike's hands, and Morrison accepted the offer. Pike was furnished with the details of the agreement Morrison had with La Lande, an inventory of the goods La Lande had taken, and a statement of the amount to be collected from the scoundrelly Creole. No reference to the matter appeared in Wilkinson's instructions to Pike, nor did Pike say anything publicly about it at the time.

Meanwhile, perhaps unknown to either Wilkinson or Pike, another American adventurer had reached Santa Fe. He was James Purcell, a Kentuckian who had been attached to a trading company on the Upper Missouri River.

From the Mandan villages [North Dakota], Purcell had been sent with two Canadian *voyageurs*, named Lacroix and Terien, to trade with Indians in the valley of the Platte River [in central Nebraska]. Accompanied by a number of Indians, they had wandered eventually into the mountains [Colorado]. While trapping beaver on the headwaters of the South Platte, they had been captured by Kiowas. After being held prisoners for two months, they had escaped and had found refuge with a band of Apaches, who took them to Santa Fe.

Governor Alencaster promptly informed Governor

Salcedo in Chihuahua of their arrival, and Salcedo promptly informed Alencaster that they must not be permitted to "return to the country of their origin."

Purcell, Lacroix, and Terien were not thrown into cells, but they were held, nevertheless, although permitted to support themselves with odd jobs.

Pike did not get away from St. Louis on July 13, 1806, as Wilkinson had ordered. But at three o'clock on the afternoon of Tuesday, July 15, he and his company pushed off from the landing at Cantonment Belle Fontaine on the muddy waters of the great highway to the West, the Missouri River. The company, occupying two keelboats, included two lieutenants, one surgeon, one sergeant, two corporals, sixteen privates, one interpreter, and fifty-nine Indian men, women, and children.

General Wilkinson did not see them off, but other Spanish secret agents watched with great interest. And the keelboats were no more than out of sight before dispatches containing details of the expedition's arms, equipment, and supplies and the identities of its personnel, were en route by express canoe down the Mississippi, addressed to Governor Salcedo at Chihuahua City.

ROSTER

Commissioned Officers
    Lieutenant Zebulon Montgomery Pike
    Lieutenant James Biddle Wilkinson

Noncommissioned Officers
    Sergeant Joseph Ballinger
    Corporal William Meek
    Corporal Jeremiah Jackson

Privates

John Boley	Henry Kennerman
Samuel Bradley	John Brown
Jacob Carter	Thomas Daugherty
William Gordon	Solomon Huddleston
Theodore Miller	Henry Menaugh
John Mountjoy	Alexander Roy
John Sparks	Patrick Smith
Freegift Stoute	John Wilson

Civilians

Dr. John Hamilton Robinson
Antoine F. Baronet Vasquez, interpreter

Of the soldiers, all but Sergeant Ballinger and Private Wilson had been with Pike on the Upper Mississippi.

"Dam'd set of rascals" was a label that Pike himself would apply to his men, and it would be widely repeated by his critics and the enemies of Wilkinson and Burr. As in the case of almost any blanket indictment, it was not altogether appropriate or justified. They had not volunteered for the western duty. They had been ordered to go, having been selected by Pike, and they had no alternative but to face courtmartial for refusing to obey a command.

If integrity and moral scruples were qualities noticeably absent in most of them, some would make up for these deficiencies on numerous occasions by displays of uncommon bravery, by courageous acceptance of their hardships and sufferings, and by unqualified obedience to their commander.

Four of them would become deserters (three of these not until nearing the end of their tour), and two would turn against Pike and state that he was involved in a plan to invade New Mexico. But Pike would not remove their names from a congressional bill to reward all members of his company with gifts of land and extraordinary compensation.

It appeared to be Wilkinson's desire to keep Pike under his control as long as possible, as if he were reticent to let him get beyond reach, and he and Pike were in frequent communication by land couriers during the first few days after the company started.

Troubles, some of them inauspicious but others more annoying than ominous, slowed Pike's advance. Dissensions arose among the ransomed Indians. The weather was inclement, with heavy rains and strong winds adding their burdens to the constant fight against the mighty river.

Reports were received that enemies of the Osages were waiting ahead to waylay them. Several soldiers were incapacitated by internal disorders and exhaustion. One, complaining of illness, was permitted to go ashore to march. He was Private Henry Kennerman, and he vanished in the woodlands. Pike made futile efforts to recapture him, and issued a warrant for his arrest. Kennerman's defection was especially aggravating to the lieutenant because he had obtained a pardon for him for previously deserting and he had believed that this act of kindness had assured Kennerman's loyalty.

Most of the Indians preferred to walk and to camp apart at night, but none objected to consuming the rations issued by the "beloved man" escorting them to their homes. The term did not denote a reverence for Pike. It meant simply a trusted representative of the Great White Father. President Jefferson had originated it, applying it to Meriwether Lewis while talking with some Indian visitors to Washington. They had repeated it in the West, and its usage had spread among several tribes.

The Indians plagued Pike with demands for more supplies than he felt they were entitled to receive. A few of them could not resist the temptation to purloin personal articles belonging to the soldiers, but Pike wrote Wilkinson from St. Charles, on July 17, the third day of the voyage, that he had this difficulty in hand.

On the same day, the interpreter, Vasquez, was "arrested by the sheriff, at the suit of Manuel de Liza, for a debt between three and four hundred dollars, and was obliged to return to St. Louis."

It was in St. Charles, as well, that in the trading post of James Morrison, a brother of Wilkinson's friend, William Morrison, Pike was introduced "to a Mr. Henry (of New Jersey), about eight and twenty years of age: he spoke a little Spanish, and French tolerably well: he wished to go with me as a volunteer." Pike informed the General that he had agreed to take George Henry along.

Wilkinson had much to say about the arrest of Vasquez, the acceptance of Henry, and the pilfering of the Indians, and all of it was critical and unpleasant. He called Manuel Lisa a "black Spaniard." The famous fur trader had dined with him on the very day Vasquez was being brought back by the sheriff, but had said nothing of the matter. Wilkinson swore he would write Lisa about disrupting "national movements" with "dispicable Intrigues." The General viewed the charges against Vasquez as nothing but a scheme by Lisa to delay the expedition. Lisa was known to have ambitions to get into trade with Santa Fe. The General promptly arranged security for the interpreter and sent him back to catch the boats.

[87]

Wilkinson's suspicions were aroused by the presence of a man of George Henry's talents and education in the Missouri wilderness, and he told Pike: "I have seen too much of the World to fall in love with Strangers, particularly men of fine . . . languages. . . ." He warned that Henry could "gain much without being made to contribute a thing." But Pike stuck with his decision to make Henry a member of the company.

As for Pike's "red companions," Wilkinson reminded the Lieutenant that "lying & stealing is their occupation, when unemployed in the chase."

That the General was worried about Lieutenant Wilkinson was apparent, for he told Pike: "My Son has the foundation of a good Constitution but it must be tempered by degrees—do not push him beyond his Capacities in hardship too suddenly. He will I hope attempt any thing but let the stuff be hardened by degrees."

In his next dispatch to Pike, dated July 19, Wilkinson made it plain once more that he expected the company to return to American soil before winter gripped the northern plains. "You may be able to guess," he said, "when I may look for you at Natchitoches. Write me by the return of the Express [courier] & tell me how you all come on . . . Farewell my friend omit nothing to give utility & Importance to your tour, and the sooner you can reach Natchitoches the better, *consistently with the necessary investigations.*"

Now, in an immediate reply, Pike set down with his pen the evidence that would destroy any shred of doubt about the purpose of his trip or that as a spy for Wilkinson, he intended to find a means of getting into Santa Fe.

On July 22, from the Village de Charrette on the

Missouri River, Pike wrote Wilkinson: "With respect to the Ie'tans [Comanches] the Genl. may rest assured I shall use every precaution previous to trusting them—but as the mode of conduct to be pursued towards the Spaniards I feel more at a loss; as my instructions lead me into the country of the Ie'tans—a part of which is no Doubt claimed by Spain—although the Boundary's between Louisiana & N. Mexico have never yet been Difined—in consequence of which should I rencounter a party near the village; *in the vicinity of St. Afee*—I have thought it would be good policy to give them to understand that we were bound to join our troops near Natchitoches but had been *uncertain about the Head Waters of the Rivers over which we passed*—but that now if the [Spanish] Commandt, desired it *we would pay him a visit of politeness*—either by Deputation, or the whole party—but if he refused; signify our intention of pursuing our direct route to the posts below—*this if aceded to would gratify our most sanguine expectations;* but if I not flatter myself, secure us an unmolested retreat to Natchitoches. But if the Spanish jealousy, and the instigation of traters; should induce them to make us prisoners of War—in time of peace—I trust to the magnanimity of our Country for our liberation . . . However unless they gave us ample assurances of just & honorable treatment—according to the custom of Nations in like cases—I would resist. . . ."

The "sanguine expectations" of Wilkinson and Pike were predicated on the intention to get him into Santa Fe, and Pike believed he had conceived an idea that would bring fulfillment of the plan. He would plead ignorance of western geography and pretend to be lost.

10

As he pushed on, convinced that his own cleverness would hoodwink the Spanish, Pike could do no more than wonder how Wilkinson would solve the dilemma he understood faced the General. He knew by the July 19 dispatch to him that Wilkinson was contemplating a journey down the Mississippi, at least as far as Fort Adams [in Mississippi Territory]. Wilkinson had told Pike to report to him there by runner from the Pawnee villages. But Wilkinson had been uncommunicative as to specific reasons for the southern trip.

The truth was that on June 11, more than a month before Pike had left St. Louis, Wilkinson had received orders from Secretary of War Dearborn to rush to eastern Texas for the express purpose of preventing an expected advance of Spanish forces into American territory.

Wilkinson was to take command of the operation,

said Dearborn, and "by all the means in your power, repel any invasion" east of the Sabine River. The orders had been approved by the President.

But August had come, and Wilkinson had not obeyed them. It was disobedience that assuredly would have resulted in a courtmartial and dishonorable discharge, if not imprisonment, for any officer of lesser rank.

On August 2, Wilkinson wrote Dearborn a series of reasons for his delay, none of which served as a bonafide or reasonable excuse. He claimed intelligence which had come to him showed that the danger in eastern Texas no longer existed. He considered it a "primary duty" to adjust his public accounts before departing from St. Louis. The civil problems of Louisiana Territory and troubles with Indians had "strong claims" to his immediate attention.

Moreover, Wilkinson told Dearborn, some Pawnees had informed him that they had been engaged for some "commercial or political speculation—or perhaps both— destined to St. Afee." Wilkinson thought the scheme had been designed to embarrass the movements of Lieutenant Pike. It called for formation of an alliance with the Comanches, and "under their protection, art, intrigue, and corruption . . . to open a channel of intercourse with St. Afee." Leader of the enterprise was the Spaniard, Manuel Lisa, and Wilkinson thought it would be harmful to the United States, for he could "readily perceive that the gold which the society seeks, may be employed to disaffect and detach the Indians from us, and to unite them to the Spaniards."

This was pure hokum, but Wilkinson proffered it as the basis for his action in canceling all "passports" (actually licenses to trade with Indians) in the Kansas area, and he assured Dearborn that Pike "would have a good look out for any intruders from this quarter [St. Louis]."

Wilkinson concluded his letter of excuses with an appeal for personal sympathy, declaring to the Secretary: "But, sir, why do I complain of such things, whilst daily threatened by the heaviest domestic calamity? For more than thirty days, Mrs. Wilkinson has trembled over the grave, and I have waited in agonizing suspense the moment of her dissolution, whilst my mind has been harrassed by a load of public engagements; and now, sir, I shall leave her, in a state of most feeble precarious convalescence, under the racking impression that we part forever. May God preserve my bitterest enemy from a similar trial."

Ann Biddle Wilkinson did not die. When the General did go South a few weeks later, he took her with him, leaving her in the Natchez home of his old friend and co-conspirator, Captain Stephen Minor, the American defector.

Only in a single respect did Wilkinson touch on his real reasons for defying the Secretary's orders, and that was in his reference to Manuel Lisa. Wilkinson believed that he and the traders with whom he was associated could secure control of the Santa Fe trade, once the road to New Mexico had been opened. Lisa was planning to open it himself, and had to be stopped. And only the man with the power to control trading licenses, the Governor of Louisiana, had any chance to do that.

A border war at the time would have disrupted the conspiracy Wilkinson had with Burr for a southwestern filibuster. Burr was already en route to the West to organize and train a force for the unlawful incursion. If war started before they were ready, the prospects of success would be greatly diminished. Furthermore, Wilkinson wanted a report from Pike on the feasibility of the routes to New Mexico before he and Burr launched their operation.

But behind these reasons was a situation which struck fear in Wilkinson and drove him to the verge of despondency.

The "load of public engagements" which he told Dearborn so greatly harassed him were not derived from the normal burdens of the Governor's office. They were pressures brought against him by politicians and business leaders who wanted him ousted and who had complained, both in the press and in appeals to Washington, about his mismanagement, his malfeasance, and his corrupt dealings. Besides, newspapers and reports reaching him made it plain that his conspiracy with Burr was fast becoming an open secret. Wilkinson realized that he was holding a poor hand. There appeared to be only one way to improve it: pull the necessary cards out from under the table.

Perhaps he should let Burr organize the invasion force and then disclose the plot to Washington, charging Burr with full responsibility for it. Perhaps he should make no attempt to hold on to the Governorship of Louisiana, since by stepping aside, he could prevent full exposure of his own traitorous activities and his own dishonesty. By double-crossing Burr, he would leave that rascal to suffer punishment alone, if the government chose to instigate legal action.

Also, he well understood the Spanish, knowing their faith in him was all but destroyed, and he understood better than any man alive the problems involved in the border conflict. If he went South, he would be able to work out a compromise that would prevent open warfare, at least temporarily. Success in such an endeavor would not only enhance his stature in Washington but might make it possible for him to extort a great deal of money from the Spanish government.

As he went down the Mississippi, in belated obedience to his orders, these thoughts dominated Wilkinson's waking hours, and doubtlessly disturbed his sleep. And from them evolved the course he followed.

The Governor's chair in St. Louis was occupied by interim appointees until, in 1807, Meriwether Lewis, President Jefferson's "beloved man," was named to the office.

Wilkinson would be credited with effecting a compromise that prevented bloody hostilities in the South, but he would lose his political influence, and the riches he had dreamed of acquiring from the fur trade and in commerce between St. Louis and Santa Fe would not materialize; altogether these were results that pleased his political adversaries and his many enemies in Louisiana.

11

In approximately a month, the Pike company traveled 500 miles up the Missouri and Osage Rivers. Most of their Indian charges walked the entire distance, but always keeping close to the boats for protection and always expecting enemies to leap upon them from the thick forests. Alarms were frequently sounded; ghosts were everywhere. At times the Osages were hysterical with fear, weeping and screaming and imploring their gods to shield them. Pike's men kept their guns ready.

On August 15, the rendezvous so long awaited by the ransomed captives took place. It was a dramatic scene. For months they had endured a living hell. They had starved and suffered brutalities, and they had seen loved ones and friends butchered and tortured to death. And then out of the forest had come not enemies but their own people to welcome them home, to cry with them for joy, and to give them horses to carry them and their baggage into the Osage villages.

Lieutenant Wilkinson had been walking with the Indians at the time of the "tender and affectionate" meeting, and he told Pike of "Wives throwing themselves into the arms of their husbands, parents embracing their children, and children their parents, brothers and sisters meeting, one from captivity, the others from the towns— they, at the same time, returning thanks to the Good God for having brought them once more together."

Pike was deeply moved, writing in his journal that the *"toute ensemble* was such as to make polished society blush, when compared with those savages, in whom the passions of the mind, either joy, grief, fear, anger, or revenge, have their full scope: why cannot we correct the baneful passions, without weakening the good?"

If no one answered Pike's question, his emotions were reflected in the speech of *Sans Oreille* [No Ears], and they were interspersed with practicality that would have been appreciated by President Jefferson and War Department officials who were struggling to secure alliances with western tribes. No Ears and his squaw and two [perhaps three] of their children had been captives of the Potawatomies. The Indian Agents who had negotiated the ransoming had been unable to locate their children, and No Ears and his squaw had come home without them.

No Ears had some strong words to speak: "Osage, you now see your wives, your brothers, your daughters, your sons, redeemed from captivity. Who did this? Was it the Spaniards? No. The French? No. Had either of these people been governors of the country, your relatives might have rotted in captivity, and you never would have seen them: but the Americans stretched forth their hands, and they are returned to you! What can you do in return for all this goodness? Nothing: all your lives would not suffice to repay their goodness."

Pike's interpreter would give him the words, and he would preserve them.

Now the business with White Hair was at hand. And an express from Wilkinson reiterated his concern about securing the loyalty of the Osages and protecting the southwestern trade from interlopers. The General instructed Pike to warn the Osages he had received new and reliable intelligence that the Potawatomies were planning another attack on them. Pike was not to fail "to enhance our personal regard for this Nation by every proper expression," but Pike was to "keep clear of any conflict in which they may be involved," while avoiding the "appearance of abandoning them."

Wilkinson railed against Manuel Lisa. Pike was to do all he could to defeat the fur trader's plans, for no good could "be derived to the United States from such a project. . . ." Certainly no good could come to Wilkinson from it, but the General did not explain why he thought it would be injurious to the United States. Actually, Wilkinson was envisioning Lisa as carrying out a scheme he might have contrived himself. Lisa and his company, he told Pike, would take their merchandise within three or four days' ride of Santa Fe and deposit it under a guard of 300 Comanches. Lisa would visit the Spanish Governor, taking along some "Jewellry & fine goods" as gifts, and would make an appeal for the Governor's pity "by a fine

Tale of sufferings which have ensued the Change of Government. . . ."

Wilkinson was speaking of the changes to take place in St. Louis after his departure for the South. In predicting what Lisa would say in Santa Fe, the General was assuming clairvoyant powers. However, in his express to Pike, he had Lisa telling the Spanish Governor a wild tale of how regulations of the St. Louis authorities had left Lisa with goods but no money. Lisa, therefore, had gone in desperation to New Mexico, and would pray that he would be allowed to introduce his "property into the Province." If Lisa were refused entry into Santa Fe, he would "open a forced or Clandestine Trade." Now Pike had Lisa's plan, and must "take all prudent & lawful means to blow it up."

If he had been in the dark about Wilkinson's personal intentions, Pike found some light in the statements with which the General concluded the express to the Osage villages. "It is interesting to you," said Wilkinson, "to reach Natchitoches in season, *to be at the seat of Government* [Washington] *pending the session of Congress,* yet you must not sacrifice any essential object to this point. Should fortune favor you on your present excursion, *your importance to our Country will I think make your future life comfortable.*

"A Newspaper has been established in Kentucky under the direction of a quondam friend of Col. Burr . . . in which I am charged . . . with an attempt twenty years ago to sell Kentucky Body & Bones to the Spaniards. . . ."

If Pike could not have known that Wilkinson was planning to jettison Burr, he could well have suspected as much. But if he did suspect this, it in no way affected his loyalty to the General, nor did he permit it to disrupt the execution of the orders he had received from Wilkinson, both orally and in writing. He applied himself faithfully to performing his mission as it had been planned, convinced that his future would, indeed, be *comfortable*. Whatever happened to the Burr-Wilkinson association, Pike felt assured that no danger would come to him as a result.

Learning that three agents of Lisa were already among the Osages without passports, he ordered their arrest. After taking a deposition from their leader, he released them to return to St. Louis, noting in his journal that "it was impossible for me to detach a party with them as prisoners."

During the last week of August, Pike carried on prolonged conferences with the Osages. Displaying the patience of a true diplomat, he suffered through countless feasts, endured endless harangues, repayed social obligations, and participated respectfully in ceremonies to which he was invited.

With fervor and force, he delivered the talks Wilkinson had prepared for him, making his major speech at a general council on August 22. It attributed to the General powers and rank that surpassed those of any other American, not excluding the President. Wilkinson was the *father*, and the sincerity of his friendship had been demonstrated by the return of the captives.

All Wilkinson wanted in return for this great kindness was peace between the tribes. The Osages were not to make war, but they were advised to send out spies, and if it was learned that their enemies were preparing to attack, they were to be "brave, prepare an ambush, and destroy them."

His journey farther to the West, Pike told the Osages, would be made for only one purpose: to plead for peace between the Osages and the Kansas and the Pawnees and the Comanches, to induce these peoples to "smoke the pipe of peace, to bury the tomahawk, and to become as one nation."

In accordance with this noble plan, it was desirable that some Osage chieftains and warriors accompany him to the Pawnee Republic. There he would summon the leaders of the Kansas; in the Pawnee lodges, the Osages and the Kansas would be in the territory of a neutral foreign nation, and one would not need to fear the other. Among the Pawnees, the Osages and the Kansas would also meet Comanche chiefs, and he would seek to draw the Comanches into the great peace alliance.

External appearances and speeches by Indians indicated general approval of Pike's requests, but they turned out to be deceptive. The expressions and the words of the Osages did not necessarily reflect their thoughts.

The French interpreter living with the Osages, Noel Mongraine, whom Pike had been ordered to take with him, refused to go. It was Mongraine's contention that he had been engaged to serve as interpreter only while Pike remained in the Osage villages. He was married into a prominent Osage family, and he had no desire to leave his home lodge. Pike thought that he "appears, next to White Hair, to have the most influence. . . ."

Pike threatened Mongraine with military force, declaring that he would not permit the "lesening" of the government's dignity by such actions. But Mongraine was not easily frightened, and he stood firm. In the end, a compromise was reached. Pike wrote the General that he had brought Mongraine "to reason, and he either goes himself or hires, at his expence, a young man who is here who speaks the Panis [Pawnee] language, and in many other respects, is preferable to himself. . . ." The young man was engaged, but Mongraine did agree to take Pike's reports to St. Louis.

The true extent of the Osages' friendship was illustrated when Pike asked them to furnish him with horses for the trip to the Pawnees. There were seven or eight hundred suitable mounts at the villages, but as if by some stroke of magic, they vanished.

Pike might have obtained the necessary number by force of arms, but the action would have brought to an abrupt end any hope of completing the mission of peace. After all his appeals had proven to be futile, he offered to buy horses, and he learned quickly that money was no less a power among Indians than among white persons.

The Osages who were willing to sell horses did not hesitate to take the fullest advantage of their position. They held him up. He had no alternative but to cock his guns. And he capitulated.

Prices ranged from $50 to $74. Having very little cash with him, he was obliged to pay with drafts on the Army. But this system was not acceptable to most of the sellers. Only a few took the pieces of paper with writing on them that they could not read.

No more than thirty-six or thirty-seven horses were purchased. It was barely a sufficient number. Pike decided that George Henry could be sacrificed, if he did not care to proceed on foot. Henry did not relish the idea of walking several hundred miles to the Pawnee villages, and Pike wrote the General that "Owing to the difficulty of obtaining horses, Mr. Henry returns from this place. In descending the Mississippi I will request him to pay his respects to you."

At last, on September 1, 1806, Pike started for the distant Pawnee villages. His route lay up the Little Osage River. In the company, as he dutifully noted, were "two lieutenants, one doctor, two sergeants, one corporal, fifteen privates, two interpreters. . . ." There were also "thirty warriors and one woman," including three Pawnees and four Osage leaders. The Indians, of course, had their own horses.

Ahead were the Great Plains.

12

Some of the indians were having unpleasant visions. "I was informed," Pike wrote, "that some . . . were dreaming and wished to return." They could see far beyond the horizons of the flat land that would become the state of Kansas, and they were looking into enemy territory.

No Ears was one of the Osages who decided to go home. Pike was surprised and aggravated. He took the guns of the deserters, and refused to let them take their horses with them. But they went, on foot. And sex entered the scene in its inevitable role. The husband of the one woman whom Pike had mentioned as starting with the company became jealous and fearful of the interest some men showed in her. He sent her back. One warrior gave laziness as his reason for leaving, and he managed to get away with his horse. The peace expedition was left "without any chief or man of consideration, except the son of the Belle Oiseau, who was but a lad. The former appeared to be a discontented young fellow, and filled with self pride: he certainly should have considered it an honor to be sent on so respectable an embassy as he was."

Embassies, respectable or not, that involved a good chance of being captured and tortured to death were hardly inspiring in any sense, but some of the Osages did remain, putting their trust in the determined, serious, young officer who represented the Father in St. Louis.

The company plodded on, across the ever-expanding plains. It was a land rich in game. They lived well on buffalo, deer, elk, antelope, birds, and fish. The Osages and the Pawnees wantonly slaughtered animals. They were in the hunting grounds of the hated Kansas and wanted to deprive them of "all the game they possibly could." Pike deplored this attitude, and as much as he could he "prevented the men shooting at the game, not merely because of the scarcity of ammunition, but, as I conceived, the laws of morality forbid it also."

In two weeks of travel, the company had reached the Smoky Hill River. Pike's guides had not taken him on the most direct route, but in a swing to the west to avoid as far as possible the main villages of the Kansas. However, no matter what route he had followed to the Pawnee villages he would have gone far from the course to his ultimate destination, the Spanish Southwest. From the Neosho, he traveled northwest and north. Had he gone straight west, he would soon have reached the Arkansas River, which would have led him to El Cuartelejo and the mountains.

The customary fall rains delayed them, soaking their supply packs and making soldiers and Indians miserable. By September 18, they had reached country in which they might expect to see Pawnees. But none appeared. Dr. Robinson and a young Pawnee named Frank were sent ahead to find the main Pawnee villages and to announce the approach of the expedition.

Around them was only the immeasurable emptiness, with no sign of human life except an occasional abandoned campsite—nothing but bigness and emptiness and sky touching earth.

And on September 19, the "rain continued without intermission the whole day, during which we employed ourselves in reading the Bible, Pope's Essays [wherever he went Pike took books with him, disregarding the difficulty of transporting them], and in pricking our arms with India ink some characters, which will frequently bring to mind our forlorn and dreary situation, as well as the happiest days of our life. In the rear of our encampment was a hill, on which there was a large rock, where the Indians kept a continual sentinel, as I imagine, to apprise them of the approach of any party, friends or foes, as well as to see if they could discover any game on the prairies."

But Pike himself wanted the sentinel on the rock for another reason. He was worried, recording in his journal on September 20 that "The detention of the doctor and our Pawnee ambassador began to be a serious matter of consideration."

At the start from the Osage village, Pike had written that one Indian woman was with the company. Obviously at least one more had joined the march, and he had neglected to mention her, for one had been sent back by a jealous husband, and on September 21 he said that he been informed by an Osage woman that two Indians, one of whom was her husband, "were conspiring to desert us in the night and steal some of our horses . . . We engaged her as our spy." The entry suggests marital troubles between another couple, with a wife willing to betray the secret scheme of a spouse.

Pike reflected his irritation in the statement that "Thus we were obliged to keep ourselves on our guard against our own companions and fellow-travellers, men of a nation highly favored by the United States, but whom I believe to be a faithless set of poltrons, incapable of a great and generous action. Among them, indeed, there may be some exceptions."

Some doubts existed about the reliability of the woman spy, and Pike decided to take action before the defections occurred. Summoning one of the alleged conspirators, "who owned a horse and had received a gun and other property for his hire," Pike told him that his plans were known, "and that if he was disposed to desert, I should take care to retain his horse; that for himself, he might leave if he pleased, as I only wanted men with us. He replied, 'that he was a man, that he always performed his promises, that he had never said he would return, but that he would follow me to the Pawnee village, which he intended to do.' He then brought his baggage and put it under the charge of the sentinel, and slept by my fire." Whether the accused man was lying, or whether the Indian woman simply wanted to make trouble for her husband, Pike had no way of determining, but he took no chances. He had the man by his fire "well watched."

On September 22, the first contact with the Pawnees they were seeking was made. A lone hunter appeared, bringing the welcome news "that the Pawnee chief had left the village the day after the doctor arrived, with 50 or

60 horses and many people, and had taken his course to the north of our route. . . ." The parties had missed each other.

However, not all the news the lone hunter imparted was good. Several Comanches "had recently killed six Pawnees, the Kans had stolen some horses," and a party of 300 Spaniards had been in the area, but for what purpose the hunter pretended not to know.

The next day another Pawnee warrior rode into camp. He had nothing of importance to relate, but as a gesture of friendship, he offered Pike the use of his horse.

Frank, the ambassador who had gone ahead with Dr. Robinson, appeared on September 24 with three of his countrymen. They informed Pike that the Chief was back in the villages, having failed to find him, and they had been sent out to search for the expedition. Soon afterward, several more Pawnees arrived, and one of them wore a scarlet coat, "with a small medal of general Washington, and a Spanish medal also."

Pike camped as the sun went down, and out of the dusk rode a group of Pawnees with a gift of buffalo meat. These Indians possessed mules, horses, bridles, and blankets "which they obtained of the Spaniards. Few only had breech cloths, most being wrapped in buffalo robes, otherwise quite naked."

On September 25, Pike saw for the first time the trail of the Melgares force that had been sent from Santa Fe to intercept him. It was a "very large road on which the Spanish troops returned and on which we could yet discover the grass beaten down in the direction which they went."

Melgares had missed him, but not by much, for the

grass had not recovered from being trampled by thousands of hooves in the Spanish column. And there was no proof that the Spanish captain was no longer searching for him. The Pawnees said that Melgares had gone home, but there was no assurance that he had not decided to wait for a time, somewhere to the west.

13

PIKE'S ARRIVAL AT THE Pawnee villages was an event of great importance in the history of the West.

For the first time, an American military force had penetrated the central Great Plains that washed on, tilting ever higher, until they broke against the immense blue and white wall of the Rocky Mountains.

For the first time, American diplomacy and politics and armed might were represented, and made themselves felt, among the wild tribes who lived at the gateway to the Spanish Southwest.

For the first time, the words and thoughts and wishes of the Great White Father were given, with official documents and appropriate symbols, to people who worshipped the gods of the winds and the sun and the moon and the stars, who looked to the Great Spirit of these phenomena for guidance and protection in the far beyond of the Hereafter.

Pawnees had known that white men existed on the earth for more than two centuries. Indeed, longer ago than that white men with beards and wearing shiny armor had come into the Great Plains farther to the south, seeking treasures that did not exist, and then had vanished into the sky. Intertribal traders had brought the Pawnees tales of De Soto and Coronado, and later reports of settlements on the northern rivers inhabited by *voyageurs* and *coureurs de bois* and Black Robes, and of other towns in the southwestern deserts in which men calling themselves Spaniards dwelt.

And in time the *voyageurs* from the North and the *mercados* from the Southwest had come to them, bringing strange and wondrous goods and miraculous weapons that talked with fire and thunder. But often these visits had been interspersed by long periods of silence.

Spanish soldiers had come, and there had been fighting, but they, too, had gone away, leaving the old trails empty of intruders.

Yet long absences did not mean that all white men had been wiped from the earth. The Pawnees could be sure of that, because the intertribal traders continued to bring tales of them. Through the hands of these Indian merchants, goods moved from the Pacific Coast to the people of the Great Plains, and goods came to them in the same way from the cold wastes of the Arctic, from the warm shores of the Gulf of Mexico, from the valley of the Mississippi, even all the way from the eastern and southern woodlands bordering the Atlantic. Horses came and guns came, and iron cooking pots and mirrors and bright cloth and knives and metal buttons—few in number, to be sure, at first; but with the passing of the decades and the arrival of more white traders, the supplies of them steadily increased. And mostly, the *voyageurs* and the *mercados* wanted in return for their merchandise furs and tanned skins and fine robes.

And now, at the beginning of the nineteenth century, the people of the Great Plains felt a new kind of force pressing upon them. They were becoming involved in the struggles between white men for territorial possessions.

Almost at the same time, out of the Southwest had come the troops of Spain, and out of the East had come the soldiers of the United States. The peoples of the Great Plains stood between them, wondering whether the most dangerous white enemies or the best white friends would come from the left or from the right.

The Pawnee villages toward which Pike had been crawling by keelboat and by horse for two months stood near the Republican River just north of the survey line that would, a few years later, divide the states of Kansas and Nebraska. As he approached, he was informed that certain ceremonies would be a necessary part of his reception, and dutiful and courteous ambassador of the United States Army that he was, he prepared to cooperate in any request made of him. He was no stranger to Indian rituals, and he understood how much of a part they played in the Indian way of life, how dear they were to the pagan heart.

In this case, another situation increased the importance of a strict observance of protocol, religious rites, and social customs. He was on a mission of peace, and he was bringing with him to the council fires enemies of the Pawnees. He could not afford to make mistakes.

The official welcome began, not in the villages but

three miles from them. There Pike and his company "were requested to remain, as the ceremony of receiving the Osages was to be performed here. There was a small circular spot, clear of grass, before which the Osages sat down . . . The Pawnees then advanced to within a mile of us, and halted, divided into two troops, and came on each flank at full charge, making all the gestures and performing the maneuvers of a real war charge. Then they circled us around, and the chief advanced in the centre and gave us his hand: his name was Caracterish [Sharitarish: White Wolf]. He was accompanied by his two sons and a chief by the name of Iskatappe [Rich Man]. The Osage were still seated; but the Bell Oiseau then rose and came forward with a pipe, and presented it to the [Pawnee] chief, who took a whiff or two from it."

The first ceremony of the reception was concluded, and the visitors now moved on toward the village as official guests. With the Chiefs rode Lieutenants Pike and Wilkinson, and they were followed by the "sergeant, on a white horse, next with the colors; then our horses and baggage, escorted by our men, with the Pawnees on each side, running races. . . ."

But the procession was soon halted, and on a hill overlooking the villages, the Osages were again requested to seat themselves on the ground, "when each Pawnee who intended to do so presented them with a horse, gave a pipe to smoke to the Osage to whom he had made the present. In this manner were eight horses given."

Lieutenant Wilkinson was sent to establish a camp on high ground overlooking the river. The Chiefs had invited all the white soldiers to eat with them, but Pike "thought it proper for one to go." Obviously he had decided it would be unwise to permit his entire company to be surrounded by hundreds of strange Indians, whose true temper he had not been given an opportunity to judge. Having lived among Indians most of his life, and having fought them in bloody conflicts, he was not blinded by overtures of friendship nor was he to be drawn into incautiousness by hospitable gestures.

Although Pike accepted the invitation for himself, he did not go alone. His statement that "At the lodge he [the chief or chiefs] gave me many particulars which were interesting to us, relative to the late visit of the Spaniards," makes it apparent that others were with him. Pike did not relate whether he was entertained by White Wolf or Rich Man, but since each was a ranking leader, both probably were present. Had he been alone, he would not have been able to comprehend what his host was saying, nor would he have been able to ask questions.

Interpreters were necessary at such a conference. Pike had two available to him, Antoine F. Baronet Vasquez, whom he called *Baroney*, and Frank, the young Pawnee who had been engaged when Noel Mongraine had refused to make the trip. How fluent Frank was in English or French, if he spoke either tongue at all, Pike did not say. But Pike could converse with the talented Baroney in both languages. Furthermore, both Baroney and Frank, as well as the Pawnees and the Osages, had another means of communication to aid them: the sign language. Plains Indians were masters of it. Nowhere else in the West did it reach such a high degree of perfection. Nowhere else did it attain such an extensive vocabulary. And nowhere else was it as expressive and as complete. Dwellers of the

Great Plains who could talk fluently in it could speak on any subject—hunting, war, personal experiences, trade, weather, troublesome wives and other domestic problems, and illness. In it they could recite history and legends and tell humorous and tragic tales. And in it they could speak to their gods.

The meal left Pike deeply disturbed, not because of any attitude on the part of his host but because of what he had been told about the Spaniard, Melgares, who had eaten in the same lodge only a few weeks earlier. Pike went to his camp above the river that night in high dudgeon, thoroughly angered by the Spanish incursions into territory which was unquestionably (in his mind, at least) a part of the United States.

But he did not permit his emotion to get the better of him. After all, he had a similar mission to complete: his own planned intrusion into Spanish territory. And throughout his councils with the Pawnees, Pike did not let himself forget that fact. He concealed his fury with diplomatic maneuvers he believed would be the most effective.

Pike, the guest of honor, was told that Melgares had arrived among the Pawnees with numerous gifts for the chiefs—mules, flags, commissions from the Governor at Santa Fe, and medals. This information was somewhat embarrassing, for Pike had little to give but much to request.

Melgares also had held smokes with the Comanches, after which he had left 240 of his men on the Arkansas "with the lame and tired horses, while he proceeded on with the rest to the Pawnee republic; here he was met by the chiefs and warriors of the Grand Pawnees."

Especially irritating to Pike was the sight of the flag

of Spain flying from a mast before the door of the Pawnee chief.

Despite the vast distances involved, news traveled fast in the Plains country, and on the afternoon of September 26, "twelve Kans [Kansas Indians] arrived at the village, and informed Baroney they had come to meet us, hearing we were to be at the Pawnee village."

Pike was succeeding in drawing representatives of traditional enemies together. He gave a dinner for several chiefs on September 27, and on the next day, a Sunday, he held a council with the "Kans and Osages, and *made* them smoke the pipe of peace."

These preliminaries over, he held a "grand council. . . ." It was September 29, and present were "not less than 400 warriors." The Spanish flag whipped in the Plains breeze above the colorful and dramatic gathering ("interesting" was Pike's word for it). Pike reached the point where he felt he could no longer tolerate the display of the foreign emblem on American soil, "and amongst various demands and charges I gave them, was, that the said flag should be delivered to me, and one of the United States' flags be received and hoisted in its place."

There was some doubt in Pike's thoughts whether he was wise in issuing the stern ultimatum. He wondered if he was "carrying the pride of nations too far, as there had so lately been a large force of Spanish cavalry at the village, which had made a great impression on the minds of the young men, as to their power, consequence, &c. which my appearance with 20 infantry was by no means calculated to remove."

He soon understood how justified his suspicion was. His initial request that the Spanish flag be lowered brought only silence from the chiefs. He temporarily dropped the subject and discussed other issues. Presently, however, with even more bluntness than he had previously used, he told the Pawnees that it was impossible for them to have two fathers, "that they must either be the children of the Spaniards or acknowledge their American father . . . your former Fathers the Spaniards have now no further Authority over you . . . after next year we will not permit Spanish officers, or soldiers, to come into this country to present medals or Flags—as all those marks of Distinction must come through your American Father. . . ."

Again came silence. Pike waited, now determined to see the question through to a finish. And at last "an old man rose, went to the door, and took down the Spanish flag, and brought it and laid it at my feet, and then received the American flag and elevated it on the staff, which had lately borne the standard of his Catholic majesty. This gave great satisfaction to the Osage and Kans, both of whom, decidedly avow themselves to be under the American protection."

Pike had won, but he was sharp enough to realize that it was an unpopular triumph and might well create dissension that would, in the end, prevent the complete fulfillment of his mission. For he saw "that every face in the council was clouded with sorrow, as if some great national calamity was about to befal them. . . ."

Pike reacted quickly and shrewdly, taking up the Spanish flag and telling the Pawnees "that as they had now shewn themselves dutiful children in acknowledging their great American father, I did not wish to embarass them with the Spaniards, for it was the wish of the

Americans that their red brethren should remain peaceably round their own fires, and not embroil themselves in any disputes between the white people; and for fear the Spaniards might return there in force again, I returned them their flag, but with an injunction that it should never be hoisted during our stay." The compromise brought a "general shout of applause. . . ."

But September 30, a rainy day, brought trouble. Frank, the Pawnee interpreter, caused a "great disturbance" by running away with the wife of an Osage. And the chief "in whose lodge the Osage put up, was extremely enraged, considering it a breach of hospitality to a person under his roof, and threatened to kill Frank if he caught him."

The next day, October 1, brought even greater trouble.

14

PAWNEE LEADERS HAD REVIEWED Pike's proposals, and
they had considered their own situation in the light of
demands made upon them by both the Spaniards and the
Americans. Their conclusions were not favorable to the
United States. White Wolf made this unmistakably clear
in a long talk with Pike.

The Chief advised Pike to go no farther and to turn
back to St. Louis. It was his assertion that Melgares had
wanted to proceed a greater distance into American territory, but he "had induced him to give up the idea."
Melgares had listened to him, and he hoped that Pike
would do the same.

Frankly, the Chief admitted that he had promised
Melgares he would turn Pike back. If Pike refused, the
Chief would be obliged to stop him by force of arms.

Pike was deeply disappointed, and not a little apprehensive, by the turn of events. He saw his hope of establishing a strong and peaceful relationship with the Pawnees being destroyed. But he displayed a bold front, and unequivocally rejected the proposal that he retreat. He had, he declared, come out under orders of the "great father to explore the western country, to visit all his red children, to make peace between them, and turn them from shedding blood." And he reminded the Chief that he "had caused the Osage and Kans to meet to smoke the pipe of peace together, and take each other by the hands like brothers." Thus far his "road had been smooth, and a blue sky over our heads. . . ." There had as yet been no blood on their path, but the Chief must understand "that the young warriors of the great American father were not women to be turned back by words."

Pike would go on his mission, and the Chief could attempt to stop him if he wished, but the Chief should not forget that the Americans "were men, well armed," and they would sell their lives "at a dear rate to his nations."

Moreover, the Americans knew that their Great Father would send out more troops to gather their bones and take revenge on the Pawnees for their deaths, and their spirits would rejoice in hearing their "exploits sung in the war songs" of the American leaders.

Leaving the Chief to consider the strong words, Pike went to his own camp and talked the situation over with his men. The discussion "was productive of many singular expressions from my brave lads, which called for my esteem. . . ."

The Pawnees adopted a tactic designed to unnerve the Americans. During the night, screaming warriors charged on their horses passed Pike's camp, but the sentinels responded with gunfire. Instead of being unnerved, the soldiers were "indignant" and prepared to fight.

For five days, Pike attempted to obtain fresh horses he badly needed for his western march, but acquisition of them was as difficult as it had been in the Osage villages. Not until October 6 did he succeed in purchasing the number he felt he required.

During this period, the atmosphere had grown more unpleasant, and he wrote Secretary Dearborn that the "future prospects of the voyage are entirely uncertain, as the savages strive to throw every impediment in our way, agreeably to the orders received from the Spaniards."

His letter to the Secretary, and another to General Wilkinson, would be taken to St. Louis by one Charlo, who would be paid $20 for the service.

In his dispatch to Wilkinson, Pike told of the "anxious days" spent with the Pawnees, how his requests had been rejected, and how the Chief had urged him to return.

"He [the Chief] told me in plain terms that it was the will of the Spaniards we should not proceed . . . he painted innumerable difficulties which he said lay in the way; but finding all his arguments had no effect, he said 'It was a pity,' and was silent."

Pike supplied Wilkinson with the type of information about the country the General was so eager to receive, stating that "Any number of men—who may reasonably be calculated on—would find no difficulty in marching the route we came with baggage waggons, field artillery, and all the usual appendages of a small army; *and if all the route to Santa Fe* should be of the same description in case of war, I would pledge my life—and what is infinitely dearer, my honor—for the successful march of a reasonable body of troops, into the province of New Mexico."

Pike advised the General that he no longer entertained the hope of negotiating a peace treaty between the Pawnees and Comanches because warfare had broken out between them in the previous August. But he was somewhat encouraged by the intelligence that the Comanches also were "at open war with the Spaniards." If he were able to "obtain an introduction to them [the Comanches], I conceive we should meet with a favorable reception. Yet how it is to be brought about, I am much at a loss to determine, but knowing that, at this crises of affairs, an intimate connection with that nation might be extremely serviceable to my country, I shall proceed to find them. . . ."

Pike's discouragement was manifest in both letters. The western expedition had not brought the success he had expected. But he had no intention of deviating from his plans, and we told the General: "If God permits, we shall march from here in a few days, and at the Arkansas I shall remain, until I build two small canoes for Lieutenant Wilkinson—whose party will consist of Ballenger and two or three men, with three Osage."

At two o'clock on the afternoon of October 7, 1806, Pike ordered his men to start for their next destination, the Great Bend of the Arkansas River.

The march was begun under menacing conditions, and he would record that "as the chief had threatened to stop us by force of arms, we had made every arrangement to make him pay as dear for the attempt as possible."

The "party was kept compact, and marched on by a road round the village, in order that if attacked the savages would not have their houses to fly to for cover. I had given orders not to fire until within five or six paces, and then to charge with the bayonet and sabre, when I believed it would have cost them at least 100 men to have exterminated us—which would have been necessary. . . ."

Pike found it difficult to control his fury as he saw that the "village appeared all to be in motion . . . many young men were walking about with their bows, arrows, guns and lances."

When Pike and his company had reached the summit of a hill that overlooked the village, he felt "as if relieved from a heavy burthen; yet all the evil I wished the Pawnees was that I might be the instrument in the hands of our government, to open their ears and eyes with a strong hand, to convince them of our power."

The passage of each mile increased their feeling of relief, but the fearful understanding of how helpless they would have been before a charge by six or seven hundred wild warriors was not to be dispelled by any distance. The Pawnees watched them, and Pike continued to maintain a close formation.

Indians he had hoped would accompany him, a number of Osages and Kansas, had been persuaded by the Chief to turn back toward their own homelands.

Now Pike had in his command two officers, the doctor, fifteen privates, one interpreter (Baronet), only three Osage men and one Osage woman, a tiny band of mites crawling across plains that were seemingly as vast and endless as the western sky.

15

Pike's route lay only slightly west of south, and it was the route Melgares and his Spanish force had taken. Late in the afternoon of the second day out from the Pawnee villages, they reached the site of a Spanish camp. It "was circular, and having only small fires round the circle to cook by. We counted 59 fires . . . if we allowed six men to each fire, they must have been 354 in number. . . ." Pike reasoned that the Spaniards had had competent guides and, therefore, it would be advantageous to follow their tracks.

The Pawnees appeared reluctant to let the Americans get out of sight; they not only continued to observe them but Rich Man and several warriors overtook them, proffering a gift of bear meat. One of the warriors stole a dirk from Dr. Robinson's saddle, and firmly Pike demanded Rich Man to order a search for it. Rich Man complied, "but when the dirk was found, the possessor asserted that he had found it on the road. . . ." Pike charged the man with lying. The situation became more dangerous with each passing moment. Pike, Baronet, and Dr. Robinson at the time were separated from the rest of the company by half a mile. Pawnee warriors rode up and began to "encircle us around." The thief demanded that he be given another knife for the dirk.

The tension ended when Rich Man drew a knife from his own belt and obtained the dirk in exchange for it. Dr. Robinson then presented the dirk to the Chief as a gift, and the three men rode on to rejoin the company.

Rich Man was back again the next day, this time declaring that he had come only to say a last farewell. He was not seen again, but the Pawnees still watched the Americans; and on the following day, five Pawnees rode in with the bones of a horse they claimed the Spanish had killed and eaten. Two of the Osage men decided they had seen enough and gone far enough. They vanished into the prairie. Only two Osages were left, a man and his wife.

Private John Sparks was suffering so greatly from rheumatic pains that he had difficulty riding or walking, and frequently trailed behind the company. On the night of October 14, he did not reach camp at all. Pike sent two men to look for him, and they brought him into camp shortly before noon the next day.

The trail of the Spanish had been lost in the tracks of buffalo, and on October 15, Pike and Dr. Robinson rode away to search for it. Led by Wilkinson, the others went on, heading directly toward the Arkansas.

Pike and the doctor were soon lost. In the maze of tracks left by buffalo, elk, deer, and antelope, they were unable to find the trail of their own party. Through October 16 and 17, they continued their search, killing buffalo and living "sumptiously on tongue and marrow," as their fears mounted. A hard rain, driven by a cold northwest wind, fell on October 17, making all trails even less distinguishable. "Our sensations now became excruciating, not only for their personal saftey, but the fear of the failure of the national objects intended to be accomplished by the expedition. . . ." A noble attitude, but to which Pike added a more honest revelation of his dominating thoughts: ". . . our own situation was not the most agreeable, not having more than four rounds of ammunition each, and 400 miles in the nearest direction from the first civilized inhabitant; we, however, concluded to search for them on the morrow, and if we did not succeed in finding them, to strike the Arkansas, where we were in hopes to discover some traces, if not cut off by the savages. . . ."

Early on the morning of October 18, Pike and Robinson set out, and at ten o'clock, they saw two riders coming toward them. They were soldiers sent out by Lieutenent Wilkinson to look for them. The company was camped on the Arkansas, only three miles away.

For nine days, Pike dallied in a camp on the south side of the river at the Great Bend of the Arkansas. Yet, it would have done him no good to have hastened his departure for the West. Winter already had come to the high plains.

Only one tree could be found that was suitable for a dugout, and the men built a second canoe by sewing hides over a wooden frame.

Time was taken for resting, for hunting, and for

games. On October 20, a shooting match was held, the winner to receive a prize of "one tent and a pair of shoes. Our only dog, was standing at the root of the tree [on which a target had been placed] in the grass, and one of the balls, struck him on the head and killed him."

Pike took observations to ascertain the latitude, penned a lengthy dissertation on prairie dogs (which were found to be "excellent meat, after they were exposed a night or two to the frost, by which means the rankness acquired by their subterranneous dwelling is corrected. . . ."), and prepared reports that he would send down the river with Lieutenant Wilkinson.

From the camp on the Arkansas, Pike told the General, "we shall ascend the river until we strike the Mountains, or find the Ietans [Comanches], and from thence bear more to the S. until we find the head of the Red River, where we shall be detained some time collecting and preparing for my descent, after which nothing shall cause a halt until my arrival at Natchitoches."

Either Pike was being dishonest for the benefit of Wilkinson or he was stubbornly refusing to recognize facts as he knew they existed. He claimed that he had "spared no pains in reconnoitering . . . or obtaining information from the savages. . . ." If that were true, he would have gained considerable knowledge of the geography, the peoples, and the conditions of the country ahead, and it would have caused a sensible and practical man to construct winter quarters and wait for the coming of spring.

Yet, he would go on a journey which no plainsman, red or white, who was in possession of his faculties, would have undertaken for love or money or any conceivable reason. Indeed, as Pike wrote, ice was forming in the Arkansas before his eyes, and the coats of the wild animals had grown shaggy with protective thickness.

He was not being courageous but foolhardy. And he was driven by other forces—by egotism, by a consuming craving for honors, by an indestructible confidence in his own capabilities, an indissoluble conviction that he could successfully defy the powers of man and nature.

He was not completely unaware, however, of his irrationality, for he wrote: "I speak of all these cases in a positive mood, as, so far as lies in the Compass of Human exertions, we command the power; but I pretend not to surmount impossibilities, and I well know the General would pardon my anticipating a little to him."

Jealousy and personal ambitions were manifest in the statement: "The General will probably be surprised to find, that the expenses of the Expedition will more than double the contemplated sum of our first calculations; but I conceived when the Spaniards were making such great exertions to debauch the Minds of our Savages, economy might be very improperly applied . . . and when I advert to the expenses of my *TWO* voyages—which I humbly conceive might be compared with the *ONE* performed by Captains Lewis & Clark—and the appropriations made for *THEIRS*—I feel a consciousness, that it is impossible for the most rigid to censure my accounts.

"Should the fortune of War at length have honored me with a Company, I hope the General will recollect his promise to me, and have my command attached to it, and on my arrival I shall take the liberty of soliciting his influence, that they may obtain the same, or similar rewards, to those who accompanied Capt. Lewis. . . ."

Pike's jealousy of Lewis and Clark was made manifest several times in his correspondence and journals. In his own eyes, he saw himself as deserving of the considerations they received and the advantages given them. He believed that his record as a soldier in combat, his wilderness experience, and his knowledge and understanding of Indians made him fully as qualified as either of them to lead any type of expedition. And he resented the generosity of the government in assigning to them a strong company, well-armed and well-supplied, while he had been obliged to undertake journeys that he felt to be equally as important as theirs with a handful of men and inadequate equipment and supplies.

Pike's egotism and his craving for honors and fame blinded him to certain realities. Or, if he did see these realities, he refused to recognize them. But obscuring his vision to an even greater extent was his inordinate loyalty to General Wilkinson. The assets to which he could make just claim—record, knowledge, and experience—were far outweighed by his liabilities.

Pike was unwilling to take into consideration factors that set the Lewis and Clark Expedition apart from any other project of the kind. It had been a dream of Thomas Jefferson long before he had become President. He had selected Captain Lewis, whom he greatly admired, to command it. Because of the dangers involved, a second officer was wanted, and Lewis had chosen Captain William Clark, with whom he had campaigned in the West. Both Lewis and Clark were officers of great experience, proven leaders of men, and long familiar with the perils of the frontier.

No soldier was ordered to go with them. They

selected the members of their company with as much care as possible. And Mr. Jefferson not only ordered and planned the journey but wrote lengthy instructions in which he clearly enumerated its purposes, its duties, and its objectives. He advised the governments of Great Britain, France, and Spain that it was being undertaken. Federal funds were appropriated for it.

Pike was not naïve. He was as fully conscious of these facts as he was that his own journeys had been ordered by one man, a man who actually had no authority to send out any military, scientific, diplomatic, or exploring expedition without the sanction of the government, which must be held responsible for any unfavorable situation that might develop as a result. It was something that simply was not done. Yet, Wilkinson had done it, several times. He had sent his lieutenant-son to establish a fort at the mouth of the Platte River (which he really planned to use as a fur trading post) and had been severely reprimanded for the unauthorized action. But that had not stopped him. He had sent spies to Texas, and he had sent out Lieutenants Peter and Pike.

Pike fully understood that the Lewis and Clark Expedition was well organized, well equipped, well supplied because they had the time, the money, and the orders to make it all of those things. He fully understood that he had been sent out without adequate preparations, without the prerogative of screening his men, without adequate or proper equipment, without funds to purchase the supplies he would need because he did not represent the national government, because his missions were not conducted in the national interest but designed to serve the selfish ends of his commander, and because Wilkinson had no wish to undertake the projects with the customary procedures (through the cumbersome machinery of the White House, the State Department, the War Department and the Department of Indian Affairs). In moving his proposals through regulation channels, Wilkinson might well have been handicapped, or even completely thwarted; and Pike knew that, too.

But Pike displayed no hesitancy in accepting the assignments under existing conditions. If he complained prior to his departures about the circumstances under which he was forced to operate, he made no record of it. On the other hand, he cooperated enthusiastically in Wilkinson's schemes, and he made every effort to carry them out.

Courage was the only characteristic Pike had in common with Lewis and Clark. But Lewis and Clark were cautious, thorough, trustworthy, and dedicated, and Pike was impulsive, over-confident, careless, and foolhardy. As for his dedication, it was more to himself and to his ambitions than to anything else. His claim to unqualified patriotism, which he so often voiced, fell of its own weight. [These are harsh charges, but not unduly so. Full substantiation of them may be found in the correspondence and official documents pertaining to the expeditions, and especially in the journals of the men who led them. The *Journals of Lewis and Clark* were monotonous in their detail, painstakingly prepared, objective, of great military value, and contributed immeasurably to geographical and scientific knowledge. The *Journals of Zebulon M. Pike* were poorly organized, unreliable, deceptive, inaccurate, carelessly prepared, lacking in essential details, scientifically and geographically incorrect, and in many places completely dishonest.]

The parting of Lieutenants Wilkinson and Pike at the Great Bend of the Arkansas was anything but pleasant. Wilkinson was angered by the conditions under which he was obliged to leave, and two days before his departure he handed Pike a caustic letter. "Before we separate and perhaps forever," it said, "I have taken the liberty to propose a few questions, relative, to the Equipment, and the Command you have given me. If you should think this a freedom, inconsistent with the principles of subordination, or unprecedented; you will please to excuse the error & attribute it to ignorance, not to a want of respect for your opinion, but to a want of confidence in my own."

Lieutenant Wilkinson, thereupon, did not hesitate to say that he thought he had neither sufficient men nor ammunition and equipment to make a successful descent of the Arkansas through various dangerous tribes, some of whom were known to be friendly to the Spanish. He considered a traverse of the river "an object of as much importance to our Executive, as one of Red river . . . perhaps more so," especially since it was known to them that a survey and an ascent of the Red River from its mouth already had been undertaken.

Nastily, he told Pike that "your reflections, when at the Source of red river, would be more pleasant, when you considered, that by the gift of a Broad ax, adz & drawing Knife—of which you have two & more setts—you prevented a Friend and Brother Soldiers wintering without stores or any thing comfortable . . . if you should add [Private] Stout to my command—who you informed me is a ruff carpenter—I should not anticipate the difficulties I now do, or dread wintering without cabins. . . ."

Pike did not reply to the letter, but on the back of it he scribbled: ". . . I will only remark that I furnished a Tent, Broad Ax, Adz and Drawing Knife and that Lt. Wilkinson had with him 19 lb. powder and 39 lb. Lead and Ball, with 4 Doz. Cartridges, when my whole party had not more than 35 lb. of powder, 40 lb. of Lead and 10 Doz. Cartridges: also that one of the men was a carpenter by profession and another a mill wright. As to his observations as it respects the Indians, they require a different Notice."

Wilkinson did not stop with the complaint to Pike. He wanted his father to know of his situation, and he wrote him: "I am now about undertaking a voyage perhaps more illy equipped than any other Officer, who ever was on Command, in point of Stores, Ammunition, Boats & Men.

"I have a small skin canoe, of 10 feet in length, with a wooden one of the same length capable to carry one man and his baggage—not more I believe—I have 5 men, whose strength is insufficient to draw up my skin canoe to dry—and which must necessarily spoil.* I have no grease to pay the seams of my canoe, and was obliged to use my candles, mixed with ashes, for that purpose. My men have no winter cloathing, and two of them no Blankets. I must

* The men assigned to Wilkinson were Sergeant Ballinger and Privates John Boley, Samuel Bradley, Solomon Huddlestone, and John Wilson. Huddleston, Boley, and Bradley would desert early in February at the post which was located about twenty miles above the mouth of the Arkansas River.

necessarily have the men wading half the day, as the water opposite here is not ankle deep. I shall pass the Republican pawnees, the most rascally nation I know—and perhaps meet with the Pawnee Pickees a nation of whom I have considerable apprehension. . . .

"The river is now full of ice, so much so that I dare not put in my canoes—last night we had a considerable fall of snow. I asked only 6 men & could not get them.

"Believe me, that I sacredly write the truth, with a coolness & deliberation I never before have done. . . ."

It was the letter of a resentful and frightened young man. Lieutenant Wilkinson entrusted it to Pike, indicating a despondent conviction that neither he nor any of his men would survive the journey. He did not show the letter to Pike, obviously realizing the seriousness of his insubordination, and he wrote on it: "Lt. Pike will please give this to the Genl. only."

His wish to spare his ailing mother from unnecessary concern was made apparent in a third short note he addressed to "General or Mrs. Wilkinson, Natchitoches." In it he said that while his prospects were not as favorable as he would have liked, he looked "forward to a pleasant voyage, tho it may be a tedious one . . . My health is perfectly good, and my greatest care shall be to preserve it. I may now and then be a little wet, but I have a large store of thick winter clothing, and a warm Tent. My coffee and tea is still on hand, as are all my herbs & medicines, none of which I have yet used. You must not look for me Till Spring. . . ."

This message of thoughtful kindness also was given to Pike. But neither the General nor Mrs. Wilkinson would see the letters. They would be taken from Pike by the Spanish.

After breakfast on October 28, Pike started most of the men who would go west with him, while he, Dr. Robinson, Baronet, and one soldier waited to see Lieutenant Wilkinson depart, "which he did at ten o'clock, having one skin canoe, made of four buffalo skins and two elk skins; this held three men besides himself and one Osage. In his wooden canoe were one soldier, one Osage and their baggage; one soldier marched on shore. We parted with 'God bless you' from both parties; they appeared to sail very well. . . ." [Lieutenant Wilkinson and his men did anything but sail "very well." The winter trip down the Arkansas was an almost continuous battle with low water and ice. Their sufferings were extreme. The reports that the lieutenant finally prepared were almost without value. Toward the end of the grueling journey, he became seriously ill. He did not reach his father until early spring. His mother had died. While he and his men were the first Americans to descend the Arkansas from as high up its course as the Great Bend, it was an accomplishment of dubious significance.]

At dusk on October 28, 1806, sixteen men ate buffalo liver and marrow in a camp at the confluence of the Pawnee and Arkansas Rivers, fourteen miles above the place where they had said farewell to Lieutenant Willkinson. Besides Pike, Dr. Robinson, and Baronet, they were the soldiers Meek, Jackson, Carter, Gordon, Miller, Mountjoy, Sparks, Stoute, Brown, Daugherty, Menaugh, Roy, and Smith.

It was cold. Snow whitened the empty plains that

swept away on every side, and ice imprisoned the waters of the rivers.

They were on their way to the western mountains and Spanish territory—on one of the most poorly equipped, ill-timed, injudicious, harebrained, daring ventures ever undertaken in western America.

16

*These vast plains of the western hemisphere, may be-
come in time equally celebrated as the sandy deserts of
Africa . . .*

WITH THESE WORDS, Pike opened the controversy about
the Great American Desert, and it would rage until after
the Civil War.

But the term *desert* could hardly have been appli-
cable to the immense short-grass plains of far-western
Kansas as he saw them in that early November of 1806.
Over the snowy sweeps drifted great herds of game
—buffalo, deer, elk, antelope pursued by coyotes, cougars,
and bands of wolves. One afternoon they "discovered the
north side of the river to be covered with animals; which,
when we came to them proved to be buffalo cows and
calves. I do not think it an exaggeration to say there were
3,000 in one view . . . I will not attempt to describe the
droves of animals we now saw . . . suffice it to say, that
the face of the prairie was covered with them . . . their
numbers exceeded imagination."

And now, for the first time, they saw wild horses, at the beginning sighting only a few scattered among the buffalo, but on one occasion seeing a herd of them. Dr. Robinson and Baronet went with Pike to gain a closer view, and "when within a quarter of a mile, they discovered us, and came immediately up near us, making the earth tremble under them . . . [as] a charge of cavalry. They stopt and gave us an opportunity to view them, among them were some very beautiful bays, blacks and greys, and indeed of all colors." But several chases demonstrated the futility of attempting to catch any of them. They easily outran the fleetest of the company's horses.

They "feasted sumptiously" on the wild meat as, day after day, they followed the tracks of Melgares and his troops. The Spanish force appeared to have grown larger as it moved westward. At one camp site, they saw evidence of "96 fires, from which a reasonable conclusion might be drawn, that there were from 6 to 700 men."

The country grew rougher, gashed with arroyos, the main river and the tributary streams narrow and crooked. The men suffered, the cold biting through their cotton uniforms, light underwear, and worn moccasins, their shoddy blankets and with even the few tanned skins they had obtained failing to halt penetration of icy winds at night.

Tracks of Indian parties were numerous, some being fresh; but only a distant lone rider was sighted, and he vanished before he could be overtaken.

They were in El Cuartelejo, and on November 11, they entered the land that would become the state of Colorado.

Their horses were playing out. Two had to be abandoned. Pike knew discouragement, but entertained no thought of turning back. Even though he found "the impossibility of performing the voyage in the time proposed, I determined to spare no pains to accomplish every object even should it oblige me to spend another winter in the desert."

The statement was a tribute from himself to his own courage. He had never been bashful about interjecting a few words of self-praise in his notes. But in this instance his words were also deceptive. He had known all along that he could not avoid spending a winter on what he chose to term his "voyage." He was aware of the great distances he must travel. He was aware of conditions he would face. He was aware of the perils of the journey.

With these realizations, which he certainly must have held when he was at the Pawnee villages (if not long before that time), it was no less than amazing that he did not attempt to make better preparations for the long and hazardous expedition. But that would not have been like Pike—Pike the undaunted, Pike the supreme, whose inordinate self-confidence inspired the conviction that he needed to give little or no heed to concerns which beset other mortals. It would have been to his credit, however, if he had given a bit more consideration to the welfare of his men, to the protection of soldiers who had been forced by orders to accompany him and who did not see themselves as superhuman.

At two o'clock on the afternoon of Saturday, November 15, Pike looked through his spy glass and thought he could make out a mountain ahead. It "appeared like a small blue cloud." Half an hour later no glass was needed to see the peaks. The men "with one accord gave three cheers to the Mexican mountains."

Pike's inexperience with the clear atmosphere of the high country gave him false impressions of distances. They traveled through the next two days, but the mountains seemed to be no closer. The fact was that they had sighted the towering Front Range from 100 miles away.

Another horse died, and several others were dangerously weak. The grass was becoming poor, and fearing that game would become scarce, they stopped to hunt. Buffalo were still to be found, and they "killed without mercy" seventeen, "and wounded at least twenty more." On November 19, they had a "general feast of marrow bones; 136 of them, furnishing the repast." Some nine hundred pounds of choice meat were dried, which Pike judged was a sufficient amount "to last this month," and under the added burdens the worn pack horses "moved slowly," and on November 20 "made only 18 miles."

Day-old Indian tracks were seen on November 21. Pike said, "This caused us to move with caution; but at the same time, increased our anxiety to discover them." On the same day, they "passed two Spanish camps, within three miles of each other."

The Front Range stood to their right, and to their left they could see the Spanish Peaks and a small part of the Sangre de Christo Range. Pike penned the opinion that the mountains offered "a defined and natural boundary" between "the province of Louisiana and New Mexico." Thus, he was ready with a simple solution of the western-boundary controversy which the negotiators of the United States and Spain, with all their powers, had been unable to settle; at least, Pike was ready with a solution that would have satisfied him.

The tracks of Melgares' force had been lost, and the trail Pike followed, which he thought had been made by the Spanish column, was one of the oldest Indian trails of the region. It led up the Arkansas to the high mountains, and the expedition soon came to know that it was still regularly used.

They had advanced only five miles on November 22, when Baronet suddenly cried out: "Voila un Savage!"

On this frigid morning, almost under the crystal and blue wall of the Colorado Rockies, the mission of Lieutenant Pike came very close to ending in disaster.

Within a few moments of Baronet's warning, Indians ran toward them from a wood, and others rode over an adjacent rise, "as it were to surround us. . . ." The company halted, "but perceiving those in front reaching out their hands," Pike ordered an advance, and ". . . they met us with open arms, crowding round, to touch and embrace us."

Mistaking the gestures as signs of friendship, Pike dismounted. His horse was quickly taken from him. Dr. Robinson and Baronet also were deprived of their mounts. Other warriors—there were sixty in the band, half of them carrying firearms and the other bows and arrows—continued to "embrace the soldiers," at the same time stealing various pieces of their equipment.

Vigorous signs from Pike and Baronet that a council was desired eventually halted the commotion. The horses were restored, and the company moved into the woods, a better position for defence regardless of what ensued.

The Indians were a war party of Pawnees that had

been in search of Comanches. Having failed in their foray, they were returning home with no prizes or spoils to display; and they were in an ugly mood, for under such circumstances "An unsuccessful war party . . . are always ready to embrace an opportunity, of gratifying their disappointed vengeance, on the first persons whom they meet."

Not all of the Pawnees were willing to smoke with the white men, and "it was with great difficulty that they got them tranquil, and not until there had been a bow or two bent. . . ." But at last Pike was seated in a ring of warriors, and "the utensils for smoking &c. were paraded on a small seat before us." He ordered "half a carrot of tobacco, one dozen knives, 60 fire steels and 60 flints to be presented to them."

The Pawnees showed their disappointment with the gifts and bluntly "demanded ammunition, corn, blankets, kettles, &c. all of which they were refused . . . The pipes yet lay unmoved, as if they were undetermined whether to treat us as friends or enemies. . . ."

A vote for friendship at last succeeded. A kettle of water was brought in, and the adversaries drank, smoked, and ate together. The Indians "now took their presents and commenced distributing them, but some malcontents threw them away, by way of contempt."

The council ended, and Pike, hoping to move on at once, ordered his men to prepare to mount. Indians swarmed around the soldiers, again stealing equipment. An attempt was made to take Pike's pistols from him as he pushed his way through the crowd and mounted his horse, and "the affair began to take a serious aspect."

Commanding his men to take their arms "and separate themselves from the savages," Pike shouted at the Indians that he "would kill the first man who touched our baggage." His threat appeared to stir respect, if not fear, in the Pawnees, and they began to drift away. Pike led his men at once from the woods.

In the melee, the Indians had made off with "one sword, tomahawk, broad axe, five canteens, and sundry other small articles," but Pike gave no thought to attempting to recover the stolen equipment. He wanted only to get away, and he kept the company riding steadily ahead for twelve miles before camping. At night, he and Dr. Robinson went back along the trail for a mile, "and laid the road, determined in case we discovered any of the rascals pursuing us to steal our horses, to kill two at least; but after waiting behind some logs until some time in the night, and discovering no person, we returned to camp."

The Pawnees had gone, but Pike found it difficult to quell his anger, and he felt "sincerely mortified, that the smallness of my number obliged me thus to submit to the insults of a lawless banditti, it being the first time ever a savage took any thing from me. . . ."

The river "appeared to be dividing itself into many small branches," and Pike concluded he was "near its extreme source." This brought the decision that the company should be put "in a defensible situation." With that accomplished, he would "ascend the north fork to the high point of the blue mountain, which we conceived would be one days march, in order to be enabled from its pinical, to lay down the various branches and positions of the country." How mistaken he was would soon become painfully apparent.

Near the confluence of Fountain Creek and the

Arkansas River, Pike selected a site for his "defensible position."* And early on the morning of November 24, his men "cut down 14 logs, and put up a breastwork, five feet high on three sides and the other was thrown on the river."

After a noon meal, Pike, Dr. Robinson, and Privates Miller and Brown set out to climb a great "blue mountain" that rose to the northwest. Pike named it Grand Peak.

If a more useless and stupid excursion was ever deliberately undertaken by an American explorer, it was not recounted in records that survived.

* In the present city of Pueblo, Colorado.

17

Pike's inability to judge western distances was graphically illustrated by his note that they "marched at one o'clock with an idea of arriving at the foot of the mountain" that same afternoon. As the early winter dusk settled, they were not near their goal and were forced to camp "without water and extremely cold."

On November 25, they started early, "climbing over many small hills covered with cedars and pitch pines," and after struggling forward for twenty-two miles, they reached the base of a mountain by nightfall.

On November 26, in this base camp, they left their blankets and provisions because they believed they could climb to the peak's summit and return before another night engulfed them.

The four men struggled upward all day, finding the going "very difficult, being obliged to climb up rocks, sometimes almost perpendicular. . . ." And when the day ended, they were nowhere near the summit. Once again they were forced to camp, this time "in a cave, without blankets, victuals or water. . . ."

On November 27, they "arose hungry, dry, and extremely sore." They had lain all night on the rock floor of the cave, prevented from quickly freezing to death only by their fire. Their hunger was appeased by a deer, "of a new species," and some "pheasants"—mule deer and dusky grouse.

On they climbed, and Pike felt they had been "amply compensated" for their hardships "by the sublimity of the prospects below. The "unbounded prairie was overhung with clouds, which appeared like the ocean in a storm; wave piled on wave and foaming, whilst the sky was perfectly clear where we were."

The snow became very deep, but after an hour, they had arrived "at the summit of *this chain.*" Even with the sun shining brightly, their thermometer registered four below zero.

They had climbed only a minor ridge. They had not reached any part of the Grand Peak.

It stood in all its snowy majesty still at least "15 or 16 miles from us, and as high again as what we had ascended, and would have taken a whole day's march to have arrived at its base. . . ."

Pike gave up, deciding "no human being could have ascended to its pinical. . . ."

He had come to his senses, but his overdue realization of their condition and the sympathy he expressed so belatedly for his companions, whom he had commanded to go with him on the inane trip, were hardly a tribute to his reasoning powers or a reflection of an inherent fairness. He blamed his defeat not only on the belief that the Grand Peak could not be scaled but also on the "condition of my soldiers who had only light overalls on, and no stockings, and every way ill provided to endure the inclemency of the region; the bad prospect of killing anything to exist on, with the further detention of two or three days, which it must occasion, determined us to return. . . ." It was a little late for such considerations and feelings of compassion.

The view suddenly grew less sublime. Grand Peak was lost in heavy clouds as they worked their way back to the camp where they had left their blankets and meat. The blankets were there, but magpies had consumed most of the flesh. They made "a meal on one partridge and a piece of deer's ribs, the ravens had left us, being the first we had eaten in 48 hours."

Turkey Creek led them toward the Arkansas, and on November 28, they were able to kill two buffalo, which gave them "the first full meal we had made in three days." They came upon numerous old Comanche campsites. Spanish soldiers had engaged these Indians in the area more than a quarter of a century earlier.

On the next day, November 29, they reached the barricade on Fountain Creek, and "found all well."

Two encyclopedias consulted in my study tell me that Pike's Peak was discovered in 1806 by Z. M. Pike. A tourist guide issued by a national automobile club makes the same statement, as do histories used in schools, brochures from travel bureaus, and pamphlets distributed by chambers of commerce.

The discoverer of Pikes Peak is not known. Perhaps

the first white men to sight it were Antonio Gutierrez de
Humana, a freebooting murderer, and a small group
(probably no more than six or seven) of outlaw adventurers. They did not live to tell the tale.

The company had been larger when it left Mexico.
During a long swing from Glorietta Pass, down the Canadian River, and northward from the Oklahoma Pan-
handle, in 1594, a number of men, among them two or
three padres, had turned back. In a fight, Gutierrez killed
his partner, Francisco Leyda de Bonilla.

The little band of treasure hunters may have gone as
far north as the Platte before turning toward the southwest. Reaching the Arkansas, they ascended it until a
great mountain came into their view. They could have
seen Pikes Peak after passing the present town of Las
Animas. It was in this area that Pike saw his "blue cloud."

It is reasonable to assume that Gutierrez and his men
may have obtained the services of Indian guides. They
knew nothing of the rivers or the mountains of the region,
yet they were following a trail that would have led them to
Raton Pass and on to the Pecos, had they lived to traverse it.

They were on a stream only a short distance below
the pass when disaster struck. Indians (probably
Comanches but perhaps Apaches) killed them all, except
a Spaniard named Sanchez. Legend had it that Sanchez
welcomed his fate and rose to become a chief of his Indian
captors. Be that as it may, the stream on which the
slayings occurred came to be known as El Rio de Las
Animas Perdidas en Purgatorio. River of Lost Souls in
Purgatory. Local miners and cattlemen, having poor ears

for Spanish and French, called it *Picketwire*. French *voyageurs* shortened it to Purgatoire.

Pikes Peak had been seen by white men more than two hundred years before Pike's eyes feasted on it. And in the seventeenth and eighteenth centuries, it was seen by many Spanish traders and soldiers who had traveled northward along the eastern base of the great mountains to trade with the peoples of the high plains and to capture Indians who had fled from slavery in New Mexico.

Archuleta must have seen the peak in 1670, for he passed across eastern Colorado from the Purgatoire. Ulibarri could not have failed to see it in 1706, for he rested his company at the mouth of Fountain Creek, where Pike camped exactly a century later. Val Verde passed through the same area in 1719.

Even if the encyclopedias, histories, and other publications changed their statements to say that Pike and his men "were the first Americans to see Pikes Peak," it would not suffice. It has been established that in 1804, James Purcell of Bardstown, Kentucky, accompanied by two French-Canadians, was trapping beaver on the South Platte River, in Colorado, (where, incidentally, he discovered gold). After being held captive for some time by Kiowas, Purcell and his companions had made their way through the mountains to Santa Fe. They could hardly have made this journey without seeing Pikes Peak, unless it was too cloudy all the time they were in the region.

Pike, by his own statement, never got closer to the base of the peak than fifteen or sixteen miles. That was his estimation of the distance, but it probably was greater than that when he decided that "no human being could have ascended to its pinical."

Only fourteen years had passed when Pike was shown to be mistaken. In 1820, Dr. Edwin James, a member of the Long Expedition, reached the summit. The distinguished explorer leading the company, Stephen H. Long, appropriately christened the mountain James Peak. But by that time the name of "Pike's Mountain" had appeared on some maps of the West. James's feat and Long's choice of a name were ignored by later map makers.

Pike became the hero of Colorado; at least he became the convenient hero of politicians who did not object to historical inaccuracies, for the state approved application of the misnomer, not only to the mountain but to a highway and an immense and magnificent national forest.

Pike's name remains perpetuated in a great natural monument more than 14,000 feet in height, an honor totally unjustified and totally undeserved.

18

Duty called, and the dream of honors awaiting him would not permit Pike to rest. The day after his return from the abortive attempt to scale the Grand Peak, the company was again moving up the Arkansas. Pike had been commissioned a captain on November 19, but many months would pass before he learned of his promotion. It was a cold and gray day, and by nightfall a blinding blizzard had struck. Because of the storm, they remained in their camp on December 1; and the starving horses attempted to scrape through the snow "to obtain their miserable pittance, and to increase their misfortunes, the poor animals were attacked by the magpies, who attracted by the scent of their sore backs, alighted on them, and in defiance of their wincing and kicking, picked many places quite raw; the difficulty of procuring food rendered so bold as to light on our men's arms and eat meat out of their hands." The temperature was 17 degrees below zero.

When the company was forced by gigantic cliffs to ford the river on December 2, the feet of two soldiers were dangerously frozen. One of the horses, unable to endure the suffering longer, went mad and ran away. Three men spent the night searching for the crazed animal, and Pike "was very apprehensive they might perish."

By December 5, they had reached the site of the present Canon City, Colorado, and the river roared in a white, frigid torrent from a great, narrow chasm. They were looking at the famed Royal Gorge.

For four days, they remained camped there. Each day, small parties reconnoitered the surrounding country, seeking to ascertain the best route to be followed. Pike still believed that the Spanish force under Melgares had passed that way, and he was more than ever determined to find its trail, not knowing that Melgares had left the Arkansas far back downstream, heading directly for Santa Fe.

Buffalo, deer, and turkeys provided sufficient food, and from frozen hides, the men made temporary shelters and poor coverings for their feet. Creeks joined the stream below the gorge from north and south. One on the north was found to dwindle away until it became "merely a brook, bounded on both sides by perpendicular rocks," and Pike decided it was the source of the Arkansas. The thought elated him. Now he could concentrate on finding the head of the Red River, which he knew lay somewhere to the south. But that was not the way he went.

A well-worn trace was discovered, and he felt certain it had been made by the Spaniards. It led north, along a creek that was bordered by springs, "strongly impregnated with sulphur." That was not the way he wanted to go, but he felt certain that the trace would soon turn southward and lead him to Santa Fe.

He could not have been more mistaken. The trace was an old Indian trail, and the campsites found on it had not been those of Spaniards but of war and hunting parties of Comanches.

But doggedly he went on, finding "the road over the mountain to be excellent," and on December 11, he and his men were camped only a few miles from the site of the famous mining town of the future, Cripple Creek.

Still pushing north and northwest, on December 13, Pike went alone to reconnoiter, and "after marching about two miles north, fell on a river 40 yards wide, frozen over." Its course was toward the northeast, and "this was the occasion of much surprise, as we were taught to expect to have met with the branches of the Red river, which should run south east. Quere. Must it not be the headwaters of the river Platte?" It was, indeed, the South Platte.

But the trail he still insisted had been made by the Spaniards went on, and he refused to leave it. On December 14, they passed through a valley "about two miles wide," and "covered at least six miles—on the banks of the river—with horse dung and the marks of indian camps, which had been since the cold weather, as was evident by the fires which were in the centre of their lodges; the sign made by their horses was astonishing, and would have taken a thousand horses some months—it was impossible to say which course the Spaniards pursued, amongst this multiplicity of signs. . . ."

Yet a trail that had been traversed by many horses, either Spaniards or Indians, continued northwestward along the river, and he determined to follow them, whomever they might be, "as the geography of the country turned out to be so different from our expectation. . . ."

Pike could forget his scheme to tell the Spaniards, if he were intercepted by them, that he had become lost. He was lost.

He was completely lost among the great tossing peaks of the Colorado Rockies, some of the highest mountains on earth, lost in the middle of winter, half-starved, frozen, and admittedly "at a loss which course to pursue."

Going on in a circular route, they passed through South Park, where a few years later the great rendezvous of the fur traders and mountain men would be held. Another horse died, and "my poor fellows suffered extremely with cold. . . ." More large abandoned Indian camps were seen, and in one they found corn cobs, inducing them "to believe that those savages although erratic, must remain long enough in one position to cultivate this grain, or obtain it from the Spaniards." And another campsite "had been occupied by at least 3000 Indians, with a large cross in the middle. Quere. Are those people catholics?"

Pike finally convinced himself that following the Spanish trace was "out of the question." They doubled back for a time, and then turned toward the southwest, "for the head of Red river." Near the present town of Buena Vista, Colorado, they came to a stream that was "about 25 yards wide," ran with great rapidity and was full of rocks. Surely it was the Red. There was "general pleasure," and Pike, like a bloodhound catching the scent of a quarry, was eager to be off to find the source.

The stream was not the Red. They had come back to the Arkansas.

For two days, a snowstorm raged, and no game could be found. Pike decided that "the doctor and Baroney should descend the river the morning; [December 21] that myself and two men would ascend and the rest of the party descend after the doctor until they obtained provision and could wait for me."

The plan was executed. With Privates Mountjoy and Miller, Pike struggled some twenty-five miles upstream (northward again) in two days. They had reached a point only fourteen miles from Leadville before he was willing to turn back. The river was only "ten or fifteen feet wide," and Pike was convinced he had neared its source when he saw it pouring from a great mountain. As they retraced their march, the immense white Collegiate Peaks (all higher than Pikes Peak) towered on their right, and on their left was a great forest brushing against the sky that would one day bear the name of Pike National Forest.

The three men had been without food nearly three days when they reached the camp of the company. Eight buffalo had been killed, and everyone enjoyed a feast—bison meat without salt. It was Christmas Eve.

Pike gave his men a day of rest on Christmas. They seemed to be "generally content," but his own journal entries were not cheerful: "Here I must take the liberty of observing that in this situation, the hardships and privations we underwent, were on this day brought more fully to our mind. Having been accustomed to some degree of relaxation, and extra enjoyments; but here 800 miles from the frontiers of our country, in the most inclement season of the year; not one person clothed for the winter, many without blankets—having been obliged to cut them up for socks, &c.—and now laying down at night on the snow or wet ground; one side burning whilst the other was pierced with the cold wind; this was in part the situation of the party whilst some were endeavoring to make a miserable substitute of raw buffalo hide for shoes &c. I will not speak of diet, as I conceive that to be beneath the serious consideration of a man on a voyage of such nature. We spent the day as agreeably as could be expected from men in our situation."

If Pike momentarily had weakened, and was feeling sorry for himself, he understood that he had no one to blame but himself for the plight of the company; but that was a guilt that he chose not to mention.

For the last six days of 1806, and the first five days of the new year, they were in straits far more desperate than they had previously known. Days and nights passed in which they had nothing at all to eat. Men were crippled by frozen limbs. Some suffered violent illness, induced by exhaustion and malnutrition. The weak, emaciated horses fell on ice and rocks, one being so badly injured that Pike "conceived it mercy to cause the poor animal to be shot." Two more horses lost their senses and had to be abandoned.

It was during this period that they struggled through the Royal Gorge. In places the river was frozen over, and they constructed crude sleds to move on the ice. Frequently, the great cliffs closed in on roaring open water, making passage between them impossible, and the men were forced to climb mountains to escape from the chasms.

Several times the company was separated, men being sent out to hunt and to find trails through the tortured country; and on January 4, they "were divided into eight parties, viz. 1st. The doctor and his companion; 2nd. The two men with the first sled; 3rd. The interpreter and the two men with the horses; 4th. Myself. 5th. 6th. 7th. and 8th. two men each with sleds at different distances. . . ."

The Royal Gorge was passed. The valley widened, providing the welcome sight of some flatlands. Pike climbed a mountain, and suddenly the country looked familiar to him. The "unbounded space of the prairies again presented themselves. . . ." They had not been on the Red River. They had been on the Arkansas. And they had returned to Canon City, Colorado, the place where they had camped early in December.

Pike knew a "great mortification, but at the same time I consoled myself with the knowledge I had acquired of the source of La Platte and Arkansas rivers, with the river to the northwest supposed to be the Pierre Juan . . . which had hitherto secured their sources from the scrutinizing eye of civilized man."

He had, of course, acquired no such knowledge. He had not found the sources of the Platte and the Arkansas. As for the stream he called Pierre Jaun, its identification must remain a mystery. He thought it was the Yellowstone, and he would be erroneously credited with having discovered it, but he had not come within five or six hundred miles of the highest reaches of that river.

Not until January 9 was the entire company together again, and "we felt comparatively happy, notwithstanding the great mortifications I experienced at having been so egregiously deceived as to the Red river."

The more Pike repeats this statement, the more ridiculous it becomes. He had known from the time he started up the Arkansas that the Red River lay to the south. Certainly the streams had not crossed each other.

His subsequent admission that he was "at considerable loss how to proceed" reflects a veracity not to be found in his excuses for his blundering through the highest ranges of the West in sub-zero weather. The horses still alive were practically useless, and this situation stirred him to "mature deliberation." Indeed, the time for it had long passed.

But at last he decided "to build a small place for defence and deposit, and leave the baggage, horses, my interpreter and one man, and with the balance, our packs of Indian presents, ammunition, tools, &c. on our backs, cross the mountains on foot, find the Red river, and then send back a party to conduct their horses and baggage by the most eligible route we could discover, by which time the horses would be so recovered as to be able to endure the fatigues of the march."

Five days were devoted to recovering their own strength; taking observations; preparing packs; stuffing themselves on buffalo; deer, and turkey meat; and sleeping.

Private Patrick Smith would remain in the camp with Baronet to guard the bony horses and equipment. And on January 14, Pike led the rest of the men, each of whom carried a pack weighing seventy pounds, southward from the Arkansas—in search of the elusive Red River.

19

Five days after leaving the deposit on the Arkansas, Pike and Dr. Robinson were crawling through deep snow in the Sangre de Christo Mountains, desperately trying to kill a buffalo.

For the entire company, all the ordeals undergone during the month of December now appeared almost insignificant when compared with their present suffering. In their trek southward, they had encountered extreme hardships, terrible hunger, and temperatures dropping as low as eighteen degrees below zero. The feet of nine men had been frozen, and other men were on the verge of complete collapse.

On the night of January 17, they had huddled about a fire, cringing with empty stomachs and cold, their hopes of surviving another day rapidly diminishing.

Pike and the doctor, fortunately "untouched by the

frost," had set out together the next morning "to hunt something to preserve existence." All day they tramped over snowy hills and through woods without encountering game, but "near evening we wounded a buffalo with three balls, but had the mortification to see him run off notwithstanding." Night fell, and "we concluded it was useless to go home to add to the general gloom, and went amongst rocks where we encamped and sat up all night; from the intense cold it was impossible to sleep."

In the morning, they sighted a small herd of buffalo and crawled a mile through the snow toward it, but once again they were defeated. After firing eight shots, they saw that two of the animals were badly wounded, but these vanished with the others. The two men crept into a sheltering wood, "determined to remain absent and die by ourselves rather than to return to our camp and behold the misery of our poor lads. . . ." But suddenly they caught sight of more buffalo coming toward them. Summoning the little strength he had left, Pike "made out to run and place myself behind some cedars and by the greatest of good luck, the first shot stopped one, which we killed in three more shots."

They remained only long enough to drink some blood and swallow a few pieces of flesh, and then, each staggering under a load of meat, they started "to relieve the anxiety of our men." It was nearing midnight when they reached the camp, and as Pike dropped his load, "it was with difficulty I prevented myself from falling; I was attacked with a giddiness of the head, which lasted for some minutes. On the countenances of the men was not a frown, nor a desponding eye; but all seemed happy to hail their officer . . . yet not a mouthful had they eat for four days."

To this doubtful report must be added the fact that the delightful smell of roasting buffalo meat filled the bitter night air.

In the morning, "all men able to march" went out to bring in the remainder of the animal Pike and the doctor had killed. Four soldiers were unable to go. The feet of two (Privates Sparks and Daugherty) were so badly frozen that they could not stand. Two others could do no more than hobble a bit with the aid of crutches.

Once more, a decision had to be made about which way to proceed. Sparks and Daugherty would have to be left. Pike went out alone to reconnoiter. Advancing toward a mountain range in the hope of sighting a passage through it, he was stopped by snows more than five feet deep. He turned back, and the situation "obliged me to determine to proceed and cotoyer [pass by] the mountain to the south, where it appeared lower, and until we could find a place where we could cross."

On the morning of January 22, Pike "furnished the two poor lads who were to remain with ammunition and made use of every argument in my power to encourage them to have fortitude to resist their fate; and gave them assurance of sending relief as soon as possible.

"We parted, but not without tears . . . taking merely sufficient provisions for one meal in order to leave as much as possible for the two poor fellows. . . ."

For the next two days, they struggled southward through the snow, and once again knew terrible hunger. On January 24, the doctor and Pike were in advance of the others when they sighted buffalo. Dropping their packs, they set out in pursuit. The buffalo were moving slowly along the white floor of a valley, and "the doctor who was less reduced than myself, ran and got behind a hill and shot one down, which stopped the remainder." They were unable to kill another before the group moved out of range. But once more they were saved.

It was Pike's claim that on this day he heard the first *seditious* words uttered by a member of his company since leaving St. Louis. Private Brown purportedly voiced the personal opinion that "it was more than human nature could bear, to march three days without sustenance, through snows three feet deep, and carry burthens only fit for horses &c. &c." It is reasonable to assume that the "etceteras" may have been employed by Pike to indicate oaths. But the language of the quotation is hardly the kind that would have been used by an uneducated common soldier, much less by a man with frozen feet, who was half-mad from hunger and lost in a wilderness from which he did not expect to escape alive. And one would have to be credulous, indeed, to accept the assertion that Private Brown's complaint (certainly justifiable) was the first to be heard on the dreadful journey. Under the circumstances, a wiser officer would have ignored the outburst, but Pike chose to elaborate on it in a manner that portrayed a pitiable self-righteousness and a set of moral standards bordering on the ludicrous.

Pike decided that the "auspicious time" for reprimanding Brown was just after the starving men had feasted "to their great joy" on the buffalo the doctor had killed. When the repast was concluded, he "sent for the lad who had presumed to speak discontentedly in the course of the day, and addressed him to the following

[161]

effect: "Brown, you this day presumed to make use of language which was seditious and mutinous; I then passed it over, pitying your situation and attributing it to your distress, rather than your inclination, to sow discontent amongst the party. Had I reserved provisions for ourselves, whilst you were starving; had we been marching along light and at our ease, whilst you were weighed down with your burden; then you would have some pretext for your observations; but when we were equally hungry, weary, emaciated and charged with burden, which I believe my natural strength is less able to bear, than any man's in the party; when we [presumedly Pike and the doctor] are always foremost in breaking the road, reconnoitering and the fatigues of the chace; it was the height of ingratitude in you, to let an expression escape which was indicative of discontent; your ready compliance and firm perserverance, I had reason to expect, as the leader of men and my companions, in miseries and dangers. But your duty as a soldier called on your obedience to your officer, and a prohibition of such language, which for this time, I will pardon, but assure you, should it ever be repeated, by instant *DEATH*, I will revenge your ingratitude and punish your disobedience."

Since this warning was delivered before the assembled men, Pike took "the opportunity likewise to assure you . . . of my thanks for obedience, perserverance and ready contempt of every danger, which you have generally evinced; I assure you nothing shall be wanting on my part, to procure you the rewards of our government and gratitude of your countrymen." He thought each member of the company "appeared very much affected" by his

[162]

words. If one of the effects was nausea, it would not have been surprising.

Three more buffalo were killed on January 25, and the men spent January 26 drying the meat on a scaffold, "intending to take as much as possible along and leave one of my frozen lads with the balance. . . ."

The casualty was Private Menaugh, who was no longer able to endure the suffering caused by walking on frozen feet. He was left behind on January 27; and it was on this day, after marching fourteen miles through deep snow, that they camped on a brook running west. The little stream was "hailed with fervency as the waters of the Red river." It was Mendano Creek, running westward out of the Sangre de Christo Mountains, and vanishing in sands in the area of Great Sand Dunes National Monument.

With renewed hope they pressed ahead. On January 28, they descended from the mountains over a much-used Indian trail, on which were "many trees with various hieroglyphicks painted." They skirted sand hills that "extended up and down at the foot of the White mountains, about 15 miles, and appeared to be about five miles in width." Before them spread a great valley, and far to the west was another immense wall of mountains, the margins of the San Luis Valley of southern Colorado.

When they camped, Pike climbed a sand hill and through his glass could make out "a large river, flowing nearly north by west, and south by east. . . ." He hurried back to the men "with the news of my discovery." Surely, they had at last found the main Red River! It was, unknown to Pike, the Rio Grande.

Two days of hard marching (forty-one miles)

[163]

brought them to the river's bank. Now Pike gave thought to constructing "transports to descend the river with," and to building a fort "that four or five might defend against the insolence, cupidity and barbarity of the savages, whilst the others returned to assist on the poor fellows who were left behind. . . ."

No timber for the two projects was to be found where they struck the river, and on January 31, they started downstream in search of it. After proceeding eighteen miles, they "met a large west branch, emptying into the main stream," and they turned up it, traveling five miles before finding a location which was suitable for a fort and also adjacent to a supply of good timber.

The beauty of the surrounding country inspired Pike to eloquence. From a high hill south of the camp, which he and the doctor climbed while hunting deer, "we had a view of all the prairie and rivers to the north of us . . . one of the most sublime and beautiful inland prospects ever presented to the eyes of man. The prairie lying nearly north and south, was probably 60 miles by 45.

"The main river bursting out of the western mountain . . . proceeds down the prairie, making many large and beautiful islands . . . all meadow ground, covered with innumerable herds of deer . . . In short, this view combined the sublime and beautiful; the great and lofty mountains covered with eternal snows, seemed to surround the luxurient vale, crowned with perennial flowers, like a terestial paradise, shut out from the view of man."

But Pike's thoughts soon turned to matters more important than lovely views. His journey of discovery had ended, the sources of both the Arkansas and the Red

Rivers had been found—so he believed. Now the time had come for him to carry on with his other assignment.

And in the early days of February, 1807, while the stockade was being constructed, he and Dr. Robinson put their heads together to formulate plans for spying on the Spanish.

20

In his written orders for the western expedition, General Wilkinson had been careful to warn Pike to "move with great circumspection" if he found himself "approximate to the settlements of New Mexico," and to prevent the Spaniards from taking "alarm or offence." The instructions looked good on paper. Should the document fall into Spanish hands (and both Wilkinson and Pike had every reason to be certain that it would) the Governor of New Mexico might be persuaded that the only purpose of the expedition was to explore territory to which the United States laid claim and that there had been no plot to penetrate Spanish borders with a military force.

But Pike knew what he was to do, and he did it. Every move he made after reaching the Rio Conejos was directed toward completing the spying mission to which he had been assigned *by unwritten orders*.

His first move would be to let Governor Joaquin del Real Alencaster know of his presence in Spanish territory. If this did not bring the desired result (his being taken to Santa Fe), he would be obliged to concoct some other device to attain the same end.

Dr. Robinson would be the emissary. And on February 6, Pike's journal stated: "The doctor having some pecuniary demands in the province of New Mexico, conceived this to be the most eligible point for him to go in. . . ." Under the pretext of collecting a bill from the absconder, La Lande, Dr. Robinson would go alone to Santa Fe.

Pike had a good idea of his location, but he would maintain steadfastly that he thought the Rio Grande was the Red River, and that the Red River had been accepted by both Spain and the United States as the border of Louisiana Territory. Yet, if that had been true, he had deliberately violated the border, for he had gone five miles up the Rio Conejos, *below his Red River*, to build a fort on Spanish soil.

Dr. Robinson was to inform Spanish officials that Pike planned to descend the Red River to Natchitoches, and Pike made out in his notes that he expected the doctor "to return [to the fort on the Rio Conejos] previous to all my party having joined me. . . ." [that is, the crippled men and others who had been left behind].

The statement was not reflective of his true thoughts. For on the next day, his journal said: "7th February, Saturday—The doctor marched alone for Santa Fe, and as it was uncertain whether this gentleman would ever join me again, I at that time, committed the following testimonial of respect for his good qualities to paper. . . ."

The recommendation was flowery and made the doctor appear to be an intellectual giant and a man of incomparable courage. However, as it definitely linked him to the expedition, it would have done him no good had he carried it with him to Santa Fe. If that assertion appears to be an ambiguity, it will be explained by future events.

The scheme had been well thought out, most probably by Wilkinson, Pike, and Robinson in concert. Pike noted, and the italics are his, that "The demands which Dr. Robinson had on persons in New Mexico, although legitimate, were in some degree spurious *in his hands. . . .*" And Pike added: "When I was about to sail, Morrison, conceiving that it was possible that I might meet some Spanish factors on the Red river, intrusted me with the claim, in order, if they were acquainted with La Lande, I might negotiate the thing with some of them. When on the frontiers, the idea suggested itself to us of making this claim *a pretext* for Robinson to visit Santa Fe. We therefore gave it the proper appearance . . . Our views were to gain a knowledge of the country, the prospect of trade, force, &c. whilst, at the same time, our treaties with Spain guaranteed to him, as a citizen of the United States, the right of seeking the recovery of all just debt or demands before the legal and authorized tribunals of the country, as a franchised inhabitant of the same, as specified in the 22nd article of said treaty." Thus, the schemers had gone thoroughly into the ramifications of the problem.

The fort Pike erected on the Rio Conejos was not merely a structure designed for temporary protection against marauding Indians. It was a strong defense works, a stockade "situated in a small prairie . . . The south flank joining the edge of the river—which at that place was not fordable—the east and west curtains were flanked by bastions in the north-east and north-west angles, which likewise flanked the curtain of the north side of the work. The stockade from the centre of the angle of the bastions was 36 feet square. There were heavy cotton-wood logs, about two feet diameter, laid up all around about six feet, after which lighter ones, until we made it twelve feet in height: those logs were joined together by a lap of about two feet at each end. We then dug a small ditch on the inside all round . . . in this ditch we planted small stakes, of about six inches diameter, sharpened at the upper end to a nice point, slanted them over the top of the work, giving them about two feet and a half projection. We then secured them . . . which formed a small pointed frise, which must have been removed before the works could have been scaled. Lastly, we dug a ditch round the whole four feet wide, and let the water in all round. . . . Our mode of getting in was to crawl over the ditch on a plank, and into a small hole sunk below the level of the work near the river for that purpose. Our port-holes were pierced about eight feet from the ground, and a platform prepared to shoot from." Pike was prepared to stay, if necessary, for an indefinite time, and the bastion might have been defended by a few men against a strong force.

On the same day that Dr. Robinson departed alone for Santa Fe, Pike sent "corporal Jackson, with four men, to recross the mountains, in order to bring in the baggage left with the frozen lads, and to see if they were yet able to come on." He remained at the fort "with four men only;

two of which had their feet frozen . . . and myself to support them by the chase."

Eight days passed without incident. Game was plentiful, and the men enjoyed the warmth and shelter of the fort, a pleasure they had not known for months.

On February 16th, the curtain rose on a new act of the frontier drama. Pike and a soldier were hunting six miles from the fort. They had wounded a deer and were trailing it when they "discovered two horsemen rising the summit of a hill"—a Spanish dragoon and a "civilized Indian." Cautious maneuvering, with guns at the ready, brought the two parties within speaking distance. The dragoon informed Pike that it was the "fourth day since they had left Santa Fe; that Robinson had arrived there, and was received with great kindness by the governor."

Pike began at once to play his role. As he knew the dragoon and the Indian "to be spies" (a somewhat absurd conclusion), he took them to the fort and "explained to them, as well as possible, my intentions of descending the river to Natchitoches, but at the same time told them that if governor Alencaster would send out an officer with an interpreter, who spoke French or English, I would do myself the pleasure to give his excellency every reasonable satisfaction as to my intentions of coming on his frontiers."

It was Pike's contention that neither the dragoon nor the Indian informed him he was not on the Red River but on the Rio Grande, and in Spanish territory.

After being guests at the fort overnight, the "spies" departed with assurances that they would deliver Pike's message to the Governor.

On the evening of the same day, Jackson and two

soldiers returned with distressing news about the frozen men. Private Menaugh would be brought in the following day, but Daugherty and Sparks were unable to travel at all on foot, and they had sent Pike "some of the bones taken out of their feet" with a fervent plea "by all that was sacred, not to leave them to perish far from the civilized world."

Pike appeared to be deeply hurt by the intimation that he would do such a cruel thing. "Ah! little did they know my heart, if they could suspect me of conduct so ungenerous," he cried. "No! before they should be left, I would for months have carried the end of a litter, in order to secure them, the happiness of once more seeing their native homes; and being in the bosom of a grateful country." His own words seemed to increase his compassion, and he added: "Thus those poor lads are to be invalids for life, made infirm at the commencement of manhood and in the prime of their course, doomed to pass the remainder of their days in misery and want. . . ."

His journal had contained no such emotional thoughts when he started on his journey to the mountains without proper equipment or any means of providing a minimum of protection for his poor lads.

But Daugherty and Sparks would be saved, and they would live to return to the "bosom" of their country. Its gratefulness, however, was never made apparent to them. They would receive nothing as a reward for their sacrifices.

The time had come, Pike decided, to send for the horses left with Baronet and Smith on the Arkansas. Meek and Miller volunteered to make the hazardous journey, and they set out on February 19. They would bring in

Daugherty and Sparks when they returned with the horses. Pike felt constrained to "remark the effect of habit, discipline and example in two soldiers soliciting a command of more than 180 miles over two great ridges of mountains covered with snow, inhabited by lands of unknown savages, in the interest of a nation [Spain], with whom we were not on the best understanding and to perform this journey, each had about ten pounds of venison; only let me ask what would our soldiers generally think on being ordered on such a tour, thus equipped? yet those men volunteered it, with others and were chosen; for which they thought themselves highly honored. . . ." These words (a mere mention in dispatches, so to speak) would be the only reward Meek and Miller would ever receive for their heroic feat.

For a week, sentinels at the fort watched night and day for a sign of approaching Spaniards. Each day the country was scouted, but no fresh trail was found. On the morning of February 26, a lookout fired a gun to apprise the garrison that two men were approaching. Pike described them as Frenchmen. At least, they could speak French. After being admitted to the fort, they informed him that Governor Alencaster "had heard it was the intention of the Utah Indians to attack" the Americans. The Governor had sent "an officer and 50 dragoons" to protect Pike, and this contingent would arrive in two days.

With this scene, a play began that frequently assumed the aspects of a horse opera.

The Spanish force arrived not in two days but in two hours. Fifty dragoons and an equal number of provincial militia rode out of the forest. Pike sent the two Frenchmen out with a request that the Spanish commander "should leave his party" and come forward alone, and that he would meet him unarmed in the open before the stockade for a conference.

Two lieutenants, Bartholemew Fernandez, commander of the troops, and Ignatio Saltelo, second in command, responded. Pike invited them into the fort, and they accepted, "but when they came round and discovered that to enter, they were obliged to crawl on their bellies over a small draw-bridge, they appeared astonished. . . ."

After breakfast had been served, Lieutenant Fernandez launched the first maneuver of the Spanish strategy. The Governor of New Mexico, he declared in Spanish that was translated into French and written in English by Pike, "being informed you had missed your route, ordered me to offer you, in his name, mules, horses, money, or whatever you may stand in need of to conduct you to the head of Red river; as from Santa Fe to where it is sometimes navigable, is eight days journey and we have guides and the routes of traders to conduct us."

"What!" said Pike, feigning utter astonishment. "Is this not the Red river?"

"No, sir," said Fernandez. "The Rio del Norte [Rio Grande]."

Appearing to be stunned by the information, Pike at once ordered the American flag taken down from the fort, "feeling how sensible I had committed myself, in entering their territory. . . ."

Pike now suspected that Fernandez had orders to take him to Santa Fe, a suspicion that hardly does credit to his intelligence. But Fernandez approached the subject on an angle, courteously explaining that the Governor had provided a hundred mules and horses to transport the

Americans and their baggage to his palace and that his excellency was most anxious to see them.

Pike countered with a protest that his orders would not justify his entrance into Spanish territory.

But the senor was already in Spanish territory.

Ah yes, but that was an honest mistake. Moreover, a party had been sent back for their horses and injured men. Pike could not think of leaving until they returned.

Fernandez thought the feeling quite understandable, and he assured Pike that "there was not the least restraint to be used." It was merely necessary that His Excellency the Governor receive an explanation of Pike's business inside the Spanish frontier. Of course, Pike could go to Santa Fe at the moment or wait for the arrival of his detachment from the North. If Pike would decide to go at once, an Indian interpreter and an escort of dragoons would be left to conduct the others to Santa Fe.

Pike avowed that the mildness of Fernandez induced him to capitulate, not the fact that a hundred armed and mounted soldiers were in view while he and Fernandez had their talk. But Pike did have the temerity to remark that he could, of course, have defied the force for a day or two and have escaped under cover of night—on foot and with several men so badly crippled they could hardly walk.

To escape was the last thing Pike wanted to do. He justified his consent to go to Santa Fe with the excuse that he "had no orders to commit hostilities," and since he had entered Spanish Territory, "although innocently," he "conceived it would appear better to shew a will to come to an explanation [to the Governor] than to be in any way constrained. . . ."

Procedure was settled. Pike would write orders to the men with the horses and the injured to follow him to Santa Fe. Two of his men would wait for them at the fort. Lieutenant Fernandez and fifty dragoons would accompany Pike, while the others waited for the arrival of the party from the North.

Pike was aggravated by the decision to leave half the Spanish force at the fort, but decided he could do nothing to "remedy the evil." The "evil" was that with Spanish troops guarding them, his men would not have a chance to escape and make their way to Natchitoches to report that he was being held prisoner in New Mexico. Had he been able to accomplish this plan, an international incident would have resulted. Not only would the scheme of Wilkinson and Burr have been benefited but he himself would have been in a spotlight visable from Washington.

On February 27, an intensely cold day with deep snow covering the ground, the journey to Santa Fe was begun. A journey of fifteen miles along the Rio Grande, during which the column frequently was forced to stop and build fires to keep warm, took them into the present state of New Mexico.

The many ordeals of the journey, the terrors of hunger and cold, had not caused Pike to ignore his orders to report on the flora and fauna of the countries through which he passed. He would write to President Jefferson that he had collected "a variety of curiosities of various savage tribes . . . skins of different beasts and birds. . . ." Most of the souvenirs and artifacts would be lost along the route in the Spanish provinces, but two highly valued specimens, living animals, would reach Washington. Somewhere in the mountains of New Mexico, an

Indian hunter was encountered who had in his possession two very small grizzly cubs. Pike "conceived the Idea," he would tell Mr. Jefferson, "of bringing them to the United States for your Exclly. although then more than 1600 miles from our frontier post—Natchitoches—purchased them of the Savage, and for three or four days made my men carry them in their laps on Horse back; and as they, would eate nothing but milk, were in danger of starving: I then had a small cage prepared for both, which was carried on a mule lashed between two packs—but always ordered them to be oute the moment we halted, and not shut up again until we were prepaired to march; by this treatment they became extremely Docile when at liberty, following my men—whom they learnt to distinguish from the Spanish Dragoons by their always feeding them and encamping with them—like dogs through our camps . . . would play like young puppies with each other & the soldiers: But the instant they were shut up and put on the Mule they became cross, as the jolting of the Animal knocked them against each other; and they sometimes were left exposed to the scorching heat of a vertical Sun for a day, withoute food, or a drop of Water: in which case they would worry, & tare each other, until nature was exhausted, and they could neither fight, nor hollo any longer."

February 28 marked the first attempt to trick Pike into committing an indiscreet act or making a statement that would convict him as an American spy. He was approached by one of the Frenchmen who had appeared at the fort in advance of the Spanish troops and who now "expressed great regret at my misfortunes." The unidentified Frenchman quietly offered to secret some of Pike's papers.

Pike was not taken in by the ruse, but "for my amusement I thought I would try him and give him a leaf or two of my journal—copied—which mentioned the time of my sailing from Belle Fontaines . . . This I charged him to guard carefully and give to me after the investigation of my papers in Santa Fe."

They rode through a wild land of great beauty, a land in which villages and little farms and many churches had existed for more than two centuries. The tiny town of Ojo Caliente was reached on March 1, and the "difference of climate was astonishing, after we left the hills and deep snows, we found ourselves on plains where there was no snow, and where vegetation was sprouting."

Pike's description of Ojo Caliente was one of the first, if not the first, to be written by an American of a typical Spanish provincial settlement in the wilderness of New Mexico. It presented "to the eye a square enclosure of mud walls, the houses forming the wall. They are flat on top, or with extremely little ascent on one side, where there are sprouts to carry off the water of the melting snow and rain. . . .

"Inside the enclosure were the different streets of houses of the same fashion, all of one story; the doors were narrow, the windows small, and in one or two houses there were talc lights. This village had a mill near it, situated on the little creek, which made very good flour.

"The population consisted of civilized Indians, but much mixed blood.

"Here we had a dance which is called the Fandango. . . .

"This village may contain 500 souls."

Several other old towns were passed during the next two days, notably San Juan, Santa Cruz, Pojouque, and Tesuque. Pike was somewhat overwhelmed by the hospitality of their inhabitants. Frequently he and his men "were stopped by the women, who invited us into their houses to eat; and in every place where we halted a moment, there was a contest who should be our hosts. My poor lads who had been frozen, were conducted home by old men, who would cause their daughters to dress their feet; provide their vituals and drink, and at night, gave them the best bed in the house. In short, all their conduct brought to my recollection the hospitality of the ancient patriarchs, and caused me to sigh with regret at the corruption of that noble principle, by the polish of modern ages."

Pike, too, had been a long time in the wilderness without female companionship, but he said nothing of how he was treated by the daughters in the little towns on the ride to Santa Fe. However, being the officer in command of the Americans, and even though his feet were not frozen, it would be unreasonable to assume that they ignored him.

"The house tops of the village of St. John's [the present San Juan]," he noted, "were crowded, as well as the streets, when we entered, and at the door of the public quarters, we were met by the president [resident?] priest . . . he offered us coffee, chocolate, or whatever we thought proper, and desired me to consider myself at home in his house."

Pike took the *padre* at his word, ate too much and drank too much wine, with the result that he suffered an

[178]

"attack of something like the cholera morbus." Considerably frightened, he "determined to be more abstemious in the future."

The "president" priest was "a great naturalist, or rather florist: he had large collections of flowers, plants, &c. and several works on his favorite studies, the margin and bottoms of which were filled with his notes in the Castilian language." Pike was not only drunk but bored by what he termed the priest's "pedantic lectures." But he won the "esteem of this worthy father, he calling me his son, and lamenting extremely that my fate had not made me one of the holy catholic church."

Requested to exhibit his sextant, Pike gave a demonstration before the church, where several hundred persons had gathered. When the priest examined the instrument and was shown "the effect of it in the reflection of the sun—he appeared more surprised . . . than any nation of savages. . . ." Pike thought it "extraordinary, how a man who appeared to be a perfect master of the ancient languages, a botanist, mineralogist, and chemist, should be so ignorant of the powers of reflection, and the first principles of mathematics. . . ." But Lieutenant Fernandez explained "that enigma, by informing me of the care the Spanish government took to prevent any branch of science from being made a pursuit, which would have a tendency to extend the views of the subjects of the provinces to the geography of their country, or any other subject which would bring to view a comparison of their local advantages and situations with other countries." In the belief of Spanish authorities, scientific ignorance brought political bliss.

It was during his short stay in San Juan that Pike

began to understand how well Governor Alencaster had planned for his arrival. At the door to the rooms in which some of his men were quartered, to his great surprise, a man spoke to him in broken English. Pike reported the man as saying: "My friend, I am very sorry to see you here. We are all prisoners in this country and can never return. I have been a prisoner for nearly three years, and cannot get out."

If the man was a prisoner, Pike replied stiffly, he must have committed a crime. The man's English was so poor and so limited that Pike had difficulty understanding him, and he asked him if he could speak French. The man could, and did, in a series of questions regarding Pike's method of entering Spanish territory and his reasons for coming. That was all Pike needed to convince him that the man had been "ordered by some person to endeavor to obtain some confession or acknowledgement of sinister designs in my having appeared on the frontiers, and some confidential communications which might implicate me."

Pike forced the man into the quarters of his men, told them to bolt the door, and accused him of being "an emissary sent on purpose by the governor, or some person, to endeavor to betray me." He then ordered his men to seize the "scoundrel," and he drew his sabre with a warning that if the man resisted or made an outcry he would kill him.

According to Pike, a confession was quickly forthcoming, the man admitting that he had been sent by the "government to meet me, and endeavor to trace out, what, and who I was, and what were my designs, by endeavoring to produce a confidence in him, by his exclaiming against the Spaniards, and complaining of the tyranny which they had exercised towards him." Pike ordered the man's release, considering him "too contemptible for further notice," and instructing him to "tell the governor, the next time he employed emissaries, to choose those of more abilities and sense. . . ."

The man's name, as Pike would soon learn, was Baptiste La Lande, the trader who had stolen Morrison's goods, and whom Dr. Robinson ostensibly had gone to Santa Fe to find. La Lande failed to elicit any information from Pike, but he did do Pike a favor. He reported to the Governor that when he left Louisiana, three years earlier, Pike had been Governor of Illinois, a bit of intelligence that Pike thought "served but to add to the respect" with which he was treated.

During the early morning of March 3, a brief rest was taken in a village of "2000 souls," [probably Santa Cruz] and there Pike was shocked by the "conduct and behavior of a young priest. . . ." It was "such as in our country would have been amply sufficient forever to have banished him from the clerical association, strutting about with a dirk in his boot, a cane in his hand, whispering to one girl, chucking another under the chin, and going out with a third, &c."

The young priest was left to his gay life, and the column moved on at a good pace, swinging eastward from the Rio Grande. Late in the afternoon, Tesuque was reached. Fresh horses were mounted, and on Lieutenant Fernandez led his charges over the hills toward Santa Fe.

The old capital came into view as dusk was settling, and in Pike's words, "Its appearance from a distance, struck my mind with the same effect as a fleet of flat bottomed boats, which are seen in the spring and fall seasons, descending the Ohio River. There are two churches, the magnificence of whose steeples form a striking contrast to the miserable appearances of the houses. On the north side of the town is the square of soldiers houses, equal to 120 or 140 on each flank. The public square is in the centre of the town; on the north side of which is situated the palace or government house . . . The other side of the square is occupied by the clergy and public officers . . . the streets are very narrow, say in general 25 feet. The supposed population is 4,500 souls. . . ."

Surrounded by a large crowd, Pike and his men dismounted before the low and unostentatious entrance to the Governor's Palace.

The curious and excited onlookers gained an extremely poor first impression of American soldiers. Pike described the appearances of himself and his men as "miserable," an adjective hardly strong enough to depict their true state. He was wearing a pair of "blue trowsers, mockinsons, blanket coat and a cap made of scarlet cloth, lined with fox skins," and his "poor fellows" were in "leggings, breech cloths and leather coats and not a hat in the whole party."

Their condition was "extremely mortifying to us all, especially as soldiers." They were embarrassed when persons in the throng asked if Americans lived in houses or in camps like Indians and if hats were worn in the United States. Pike felt these "observations . . . sufficient to shew the impression our uncouth appearance made. . . ."

Today the Governor's Palace still stands, well-preserved and crammed with relics and artifacts of bygone centuries. Today the building's serene, wrinkled walls still look upon the Plaza of Santa Fe, as they did on March 3, 1807, and as they had for two hundred years before that eventful day in the history of the Southwest.

21

WITHOUT CEREMONY, Pike and his ragged men were ushered "through various rooms, the floors of which were covered with skins of buffalo, bear, or some other animal," but they were obliged to wait in an inner chamber for some time before Governor Alencaster appeared.

They rose. His Excellency wasted no time with social amenities or light talk, and the following dialogue took place, as reported by Pike in his journal.

> *Governor:* Do you speak French?
> *Pike:* Yes, sir.
> *Governor:* You come to reconnoiter our country, do you?
> *Pike:* I marched to reconnoiter our own.
> *Governor:* In what character are you?
> *Pike:* In my proper character, an officer of the United States Army.
> *Governor:* And this Robinson, is he attached to your party?

Pike: No.

Governor: Do you know him?

Pike: Yes, he is from St. Louis.

Governor: How many men have you?

Pike: Fifteen.

Governor: And this Robinson makes sixteen.

Pike: I have already told your excellency that he does not belong to my party, and shall answer no more interrogatories on that subject.

Governor: When did you leave St. Louis?

Pike: 15th July.

Governor: I think you marched in June.

Pike: No, sir!

Governor: Well! return with Mr. Bartholemew [Lieutenant Fernandez] to his house, and come here again at seven o'clock, and bring your papers.

Pike and his men left the Palace.

It had not been a friendly interview. Alencaster had shown no graciousness; his manner had been brusque; and his distrust of Pike had been apparent. Pike at once began a series of cloak-and-dagger maneuvers that were neither wise nor necessary, and which gained him no advantage.

22

Before dr. robinson left the Rio Conejos, he and Pike
had agreed on the stories to be told to Governor Alencaster.
In Santa Fe, Robinson would not mention the Pike Expedition. He would say that he had left St. Louis on June 15
with a hunting party and that his sole mission was to
collect the money La Lande owed Morrison. If Pike
reached Santa Fe, he would admit that he had known
Robinson in St. Louis, nothing more. They saw in this
deceptiveness the possibility of being able to operate more
efficiently and effectively as individual spies.

On the second day after leaving the Rio Conejos fort,
Robinson had fallen in with two friendly Utah Indians,
and they had agreed to show him the trail to the nearest
settlement. The doctor was taken into custody by authorities in Ojo Caliente. An express reporting his arrival was
sent at once to Alencaster, and the next morning he was
started on his way to Santa Fe under a military escort.

As Robinson recounted the scene in the Governor's Palace, Alencaster "received me with great austerity at first, and entered into an examination of my business and took possession of all my papers. After all this was explained, he ordered me to a room where the officers were confined when under arrest and a non-commissioned officer to attend me."

But Robinson was not held behind bars. He was allowed to walk about the city, and he was "supplied with provisions from the governor's table."

Alencaster looked into the claim against La Lande, and then informed the doctor that the Creole possessed no property but that an effort would be made to have the debt paid "at some future period." The arrangement did not satisfy Robinson, and he made "a spirited remonstrance," declaring the situation to be an infringement on the treaties between Spain and the United States and charging that Spanish authorities were protecting "a refugee citizen of the United States against his creditors."

Although he ignored the vehement protest, Alencaster must have been somewhat impressed by it, for he invited Robinson to dinner, and he tendered him "rather more respectful treatment than I had hitherto received . . ."

But Robinson soon learned that Alencaster's kindness did not stem only from respect for him. His Excellency was afflicted with dropsy, and he wanted the American doctor's medical advice as well as his company at table. Dr. Robinson prescribed "a regimen and mode of treatment." Unfortunately the prescription was in conflict with ministrations practiced by a padre who served as the

Governor's physician, and he had some unkind things to say about the St. Louis intruder.

Meanwhile, unknown to Robinson, troops were riding hard toward the north. Alencaster was no more willing to swallow Robinson's story than the local priest-physician was willing to let Robinson move in on his practice. The Governor decided that it would be best to have Robinson taken down to the village of Albuquerque and detained there until a full investigation of his case could be completed. To Governor Salcedo in Chihuahua, Alencaster dispatched an express in which he left no doubt that he suspected Robinson of being "sent by Wilkinson himself." Alencaster told Salcedo that Robinson stated that he had left St. Louis "on 15 June last for the country of the Pananas [Pawnees], with the purpose of making various collections of money, and intending to return to the said San Luis in four or five months, and that, having learned that some of his debtors had set out for this Province, he undertook his journey, accompanied by the fifteen men with whom he left, they having the purpose of hunting on the Rivers Arcas, Arcansan, Colorado and others, and he with the intention of entering this Province; and that in the Mountains near it the only two Hunters who had agreed to accompany him abandoned him, being exhausted by the great quantity of Snow and the uncertainty of their Route; for which reason he was forced to go on alone until he met the Yutas, who were hunting, by whom he was well received and there he succeeded in getting them to guide him and accompany him.

"This said Robinson has declared that he is a Professor of Medicine, and in his manner he gives evidence of

[188]

being well educated . . . He has given me some Information about the ideas of the American Government to extend its borders immediately adjacent to this Province . . ."

In Albuquerque, Robinson was placed in the custody of Lieutenant Melgares, the officer who had been sent out the previous summer to stop Pike and who had left the Pawnees only a few weeks before the Pike Expedition reached them.

Approximately a fortnight after Alencaster's dispatch had gone to Salcedo, Pike and his men were in the Governor's Palace at Santa Fe.

23

PIKE'S SECOND AUDIENCE with Governor Alencaster on the evening of March 3 was more cordial than their first meeting. The Governor asked to see Pike's commission and his military orders from Wilkinson. These were read to him, after which, according to Pike, "he got up and gave me his hand, for the first time, and said he was happy to be acquainted with me as a man of honor and a gentleman. . . ."

Present at this conference was a rough character whom Pike called "Solomon Colly." His true name was Zalmon Cooley, and he was one of Philip Nolan's band of renegades captured in a fight with Spanish troops in Texas in March, 1801. Nolan, a spy for Wilkinson and Burr, had been killed in the battle. For six years, Cooley and a dozen other Nolan raiders had been held in various Spanish towns.

Alencaster did not choose to examine more of Pike's documents at the moment, and dismissed him. Pike took it for granted that the investigation was concluded. He was permitted to take with him the suitcase in which he carried his documents as he left the Palace. Quickly, he distributed them among his men with orders that they be concealed.

But in the morning he learned that the hospitable "inhabitants were treating the men with liquor," and fearing that in their drunken state the soldiers would lose the papers, he hurriedly retrieved them. This had no more than been accomplished when an officer appeared and took the papers, with the announcement that Alencaster had decided to make a closer study of them.

The byplay with his papers was sheer melodrama. If he had been genuinely fearful of losing them, he would not have taken them with him to Santa Fe. He would have cached them some place north of the Rio Grande. That, of course, was wholly unnecessary because they were not incriminating. They were for the most part nothing more important than some letters from General Wilkinson relative to his negotiations with the Osages and Pawnees in territory that unquestionably belonged to the United States, letters from Lieutenant Wilkinson to his father and mother, documents pertaining to the fur trade of the Upper Missouri, copies of his speeches to Indians, his journal notes, some traverse tables and meteorological observations, essays on flowers and animals, and some crude manuscript maps—absolutely nothing that cast him in the role of a spy or that might not have been found in the baggage of any explorer.

His wish to retain his daily notes was understandable, and he was successful in saving a large part of them on the ground that they were a private diary and had nothing to do with his appearance in Spanish territory. He might have been able to keep other documents had he not made such obvious efforts to hide them, which only increased the suspicions of the Spaniards.

Pike cried about the "falsity, want of candour, and meanness" of the Spanish officials, but to no avail. The papers would go to Chihuahua, and there they would vanish into the Spanish military archives where they would remain for more than a century. [Pike was not a meteorologist, not a surveyor, not a botanist, not a geologist, not a cartographer. His knowledge of any of these sciences was superficial. When at last his papers were recovered in Mexico, they were of little value.]

On March 4, Pike had his third meeting with Alencaster.

> *Governor:* You must—with your troops—go to Chihuahua . . . to appear before the commandant-general . . .
>
> *Pike:* If we go to Chihuahua we must be considered as prisoners of war?
>
> *Governor:* By no means.
>
> *Pike:* You have already disarmed my men without my knowledge, are their arms to be returned or not?
>
> *Governor:* They can receive them any moment.

Restoration of the rifles that belonged to his men was especially important to Pike because he planned to make an effort to conceal some of his papers in the barrels.

Pike: But sir, I cannot consent to be led three or four hundred leagues out of my route, without its being by force of arms.

Governor: I know you do not go voluntarily, but I will give you a certificate from under my hand of my having obliged you to march.

Pike: I will address you a letter on the subject.

Governor: You will dine with me today, and march afterwards to a village about six miles distant, escorted by captain Anthony D'Almansa, with an attachment of dragoons, who will accompany you to where the remainder of your escort is now waiting for you, under the command of the officer who commanded the expedition to the Pawnees. [Lieutenant Melgares. He would become Governor of New Mexico.]

Pike: I would not wish to be impertinent in my observations to your excellency, but pray sir! do you not think it was a greater infringement of our territory to send 600 miles in the Pawnees, [Melgares' expedition] than for me with our small party to come on the frontiers of yours with an intent to descend Red river?

Alencaster only shrugged off the question. If he was irritated by Pike's histrionics, it did not affect his sense of fairness or his generosity. He gave Pike some articles of clothing, which he said had been made by his sister in Spain, and money in the equivalent of twenty-one American dollars. The money was "the king's allowance" for Pike on the journey to Chihuahua.

After a "rather splendid dinner," Alencaster called for his coach, and he and Pike and Lieutenant Fernandez drove "out three miles," accompanied by a guard of

[193]

Cavalry. In a desert defile, Pike's men and a military escort were waiting for them. The Governor's parting words to Pike were: "Remember Alencaster, in peace or war."

It was ten o'clock that night when the column halted in the tiny village of Cienega. Pike was traveling where no American military man (indeed, few Americans of any calling) had ever gone, down the *Camino Real* from Santa Fe to Chihuahua, the long dusty road that passed through the heart of the New Mexico Pueblo country. A most valuable part of his original narrative would be his descriptions of the ancient Indian towns, some of them centuries old before Coronado had first seen them, and his remarks on the manners and mode of life of the peoples who had dwelt there since the early morning of the Southwest.

On March 5, he saw Santo Domingo Pueblo, "a large village, the population being about 1000 natives . . . the Rio Del Norte on our west; the mountains of St. Dies [Sandias] to the south, and the valley round the town, on which were numerous herds of goats, sheep and asses; and upon the whole, this was one of the handsomest views of New Mexico."

Captain D'Almansa took him into the Santo Domingo church, and he was "much astonished to find enclosed in mud-brick walls, many rich paintings, and the Saint—Domingo—as large as life, elegantly ornamented with gold and silver. . . ."

Although entranced with the beauty of the land, Pike did not for a moment forget his duty to spy, and he was especially excited when, in San Felipe, a padre "shewed me a statistical table, on which he had in a regular manner, taken the whole province of New Mexico, by villages, beginning at Tous [Taos], on the north-west, and ending with Valencia on the south, giving their latitude, longitude, and population, whether natives or Spaniards, civilized or barbarous, Christians or Pagans, numbers, name of the nation, when converted, how governed, military force, clergy, salary, &c. &c.; in short, a complete geographical, statistical and historical sketch of the province." A gold mine for a secret agent, and Pike attempted to obtain a copy of the data, but he failed. Captain D'Almansa was on the job, and blocked the transaction.

On to Algodones and Bernalillo and Sandia Pueblo went the column, passing through a land "better cultivated and inhabited" than any Pike had seen, and in it "the citizens were beginning to open the canals, to let in the water of the river to fertilize the plains and fields which border its banks on both sides; where he saw men, women and children of all ages and sexes at the joyful labor which was to crown with rich abundance their future harvest and ensure them plenty for the ensuing year . . . everything appeared to give life and gaity to the surrounding scenery. . . ." Pike was reminded of the "bright descriptions" he had read "of the opening of the canals of Egypt."

Albuquerque might have been merely "a village on the east side of the Rio del Norte," but life in it was anything but dull. A stop was made there on March 7, and Pike and D'Almansa were graciously invited into the apartment of Father Ambrosio Guerra. After refreshments, the padre "ordered his adopted children of the female sex, to appear, when they came in by turns, Indians of various nations, Spanish, French, and finally, two young girls, who from their complexion I conceived to be English. . . ." The girls were English, and they had been purchased as infants by the priest from a Plains tribe. Nothing was known of their parents, and they had been too young at the time of their ransom to know their names or to give any clue about where or by whom they had been stolen.

Dinner with Father Guerra was a gala event, with excellent wines, and Pike was inspired to new heights of eloquence in describing it. For "to crown all, we were waited on by half a dozen of those beautiful girls, who like Hebe at the feast of the gods, converted our wine to nectar, and with their ambrosial breath shed incense on our cups."

The life of luxury in Albuquerque ended all too soon, for D'Almansa had selected as a stopping place for the night a tiny village a short distance farther down the Rio Grande.

As Pike entered the quarters assigned to him, he was startled by the sight of a familiar figure. Before the fireplace, deeply absorbed in a book, was Dr. Robinson, not the Robinson who had left the fort on the Rio Conejos "pale, emaciated, with uncombed locks and beard of eight months growth," but a handsome, clean, well-clothed Robinson, "with fire, unsubdued enterprise and fortitude."

Pike: Robinson!
Robinson: Yes, but I do not know you.
Pike: But I know you.

By no stretch of the imagination could Pike be called a writer, but he did the best he could to thrill the potential readers (and there were many) of the narrative he prepared. He was maudlin, sickly sentimental, and truth in his hands had the elasticity of rubber.

Ah, yes, Robinson finally admitted knowing him, and he had the doctor wailing: "I would not be unknown to you here, in this land of tyranny and oppression, to avoid all the pains they dare to inflict. Yet, my friend, I grieve to see you here and thus, for I presume you are a prisoner."

"No!" Pike cried. "I wear my sword you see, and all my men have their arms, and the moment they dare to ill treat us we will surprise their guards in the night, carry off some horses and make our way to the Appaches and set them at defiance."

Enter Captain D'Almansa.

Pike, carrying the scene to ridiculous lengths, introduced the doctor to the captain as his "companion de voyage and friend." D'Almansa's expression indicated that he resented Pike's attempt to make a fool of him. Robinson, much more clever when it came to intrigue and a much more capable actor than Pike, then admitted that D'Almansa knew the truth of things. The doctor, seeing no advantage and possible harm in continuing the deception, had admitted to Lieutenant Melgares that he had come West as a member of the Pike Expedition.

Pike, of course, was once again "mortified," and he made haste to explain his lying in a letter to Governor Alencaster. Dr. Robinson had left St. Louis with him, he confessed, and "on our arrival on the Rio del Norte—then supposed Red river—he left the party in order to come to Santa Fe, with a view to obtaining information as to trade, and collect some debts due to persons in the Illinois. On my being informed of his embarrassments, I conceived it would be adding to them, to acknowledge his having accompanied a military party on to the frontier of the province, and conceived myself bound in honor and friendship to conceal it; but his scorning any longer the disguise he had assumed, has left me at liberty to make this acknowledgement to your excellency, which I hope will sufficiently exculpate me in the opinion of every man of honor, and of the world, for having denied a fact, when I conceived the safety of a friend, in a foreign country, was concerned in the event. The above statement will be corroborated by general Wilkinson, and he will be reclaimed by the United States as a citizen, agreeably to our treaties with Spain, regulating the intercourse, commerce, &c. between the two nations. . . ." Even in his confession, Pike could not "conceive" to be honest, and his continued prevarifications would long react against him.

Almost at the same time, in New Orleans, General Wilkinson was writing Secretary Dearborn that God had spared his son, but that he had heard "nothing of Lt. Pike & have some fears for Him, as his Route would approximate to St. Afee—yet the Severity of the Season may have arrested his movement." Even Dearborn, who had never seen the West, was not stupid enough to believe that a company which left St. Louis on July 15, on a route that would "approximate St. Afee," could get to Natchitoches before cold weather. Lieutenant Wilkinson, who had left the Great Bend of the Arkansas on October 28, had not been able to accomplish that feat.

Senoritas, good wines, violin music, and dancing—not the severity of the season—were occupying the attention of Dr. Robinson, Pike, and the soldiers in the village of "tousac, hard by the Rio Grande south of Albuquerque."

On March 8, the column reached San Fernandez.

Awaiting them there were Lieutenant Melgares and the troops that would take them on to Chihuahua.

At last the two lieutenants had met—the backwoods soldier, arrogant, egotistical, filled with self-righteousness, proclaiming too loudly and too often his moral sentiments, and the aristocratic soldier, born of a good family in Spain, polished and sophisticated. If they had anything in common it was raw courage—that alone.

Pike soon came to understand, as he admitted, that the man who had attempted to hunt him down on the Pawnee plains was not a roughneck frontier fighter but a gentleman, well-educated and "possessing none of the haughty Castilian pride, but much of the urbanity of a Frenchman," an officer of integrity and honor.

And on that afternoon of March 8, Melgares also showed himself to be a gracious and considerate host. To the *alcaldes* of several small villages adjacent to San Fernandez he sent similar notes: "Send this evening six or eight of your handsomest young girls . . . I propose giving a fandango for the entertainment of the American officers arrived this day."

Pike was both unappreciative and rudely critical of Melgares' efforts to entertain him, expressing the view that the order for the girls, which was promptly obeyed, portrayed "more clearly than a chapter of observations, the degraded state of the common people." But he had to admit "there was really a handsome display of beauty."

24

COMMANDANT-GENERAL AND GOVERNOR NEMESIO SALCEDO was a polite man of medium stature, who gave the appearance of having on his shoulders all the problems he could bear. His jurisdiction was several times as large as his native Spain; indeed, its borders, except those created by the sea and Spanish provinces to the south, were either disputed by the United States or actually unknown. For years, war with the Americans over the issues of the frontiers had appeared inescapable, and on more than one occasion, troops of the two nations had drawn lines of combat. That a bloody conflict had not occurred may have been, as some said, a miracle performed by the Lord, but Salcedo was not willing to overlook the possibility that political and military deals (not all of which were advantageous to Spain, by any means) had much to do with the present stalemate.

It was Governor Salcedo's private opinion that Lewis and Clark had invaded Spanish territory. He had issued orders that no more American expeditions (scientific or any other kind) were to be permitted to advance up the rivers running from the Rocky Mountains and the Great Plains to the Mississippi; and he had urged provincial executives such as Alencaster to make every effort to win interior tribes to the banner of Spain through trading missions, gifts, hospitality, commissions, medals, titles, or any other means deemed advisable by them.

To the politically powerful Marques de Casa Calvo, who had been one of the King's commissioners for the transfer of Louisiana Territory to the United States, Salcedo had written a strongly worded letter about American exploration of the West. The Marques had consented to let an American expedition, commanded by William Dunbar, ascend the Red and Arkansas River on the ground that it was "purely Geographical and scientific," and Salcedo had rebuked him for issuing passports to its members. The expedition was, declared Salcedo, "both unnecessary and dangerous to the Interests of our Government . . . The results for Geography and other sciences are unnecessary because we are in possession of thorough knowledge of the said Rivers from their sources to their confluence with the Misisipi, as well as the lands which lie between the two. . . ." Salcedo looked upon all scientific expeditions as primarily spying operations, and he warned the Marques that any information they obtained could be put to "dangerous use in the Future, in the case of hostilities between Spain and the United States."

But not only border and military questions beset

Salcedo. Civic, economic and legal burdens also weighed constantly upon him. And not only Apaches and Comanches wanted his scalp, but countless political enemies as well, among whom were some close to the Spanish Court. He was a harried and worn man.

Then early in 1806, word had come from agents in St. Louis that a military company led by Lieutenant Zebulon Montgomery Pike would be sent by the veteran Spanish spy, General James Wilkinson, a crony of the ambitious filibusterer, Aaron Burr, to explore the Arkansas and Red Rivers and negotiate pacts with Indian tribes for the purpose of making them allies of the United States.

Quickly Salcedo had sent Melgares with a strong force to stop Pike, but Melgares had missed him, and Pike had turned up in Santa Fe. Alencaster had relieved himself of the touchy problem by sending Pike on to Chihuahua. And there Pike was, outside in the hall. The day was Thursday, April 2, 1807.

Let him cool his heels for a time, Salcedo ordered, and send in Lieutenant Melgares. Also, summon Juan Pedro Walker. Melgares would divulge what he had learned about Pike's spying, which was probably very little. Walker would be useful in several ways, being a man of scientific attainments and a linguist.

Juan Pedro Walker, born in New Orleans of an English father and a French mother, had studied surveying and had been engaged in establishing the boundary between the United States and the Gulf Coast possessions of Spain. He spoke English, French, and Spanish with fluency. When Louisiana became American territory, he had left his native country and had become a Spanish citizen. He had conducted surveys for the Spanish government in Texas, and had been commissioned an officer in the Spanish cavalry. But his greatest value was as a translator and interpreter.

When Pike was ushered before him, Salcedo maintained a stern countenance. "Be seated," he said. "You have given us and yourself a great deal of trouble."

"On my part entirely unsought," said Pike, "and on that of the Spanish Government voluntary."

"Where are your papers?"

"Under the charge of lieutenant Melgares."

Melgares produced Pike's battered document case. Walker not only acted as interpreter but explained the nature of each paper as it was placed before Salcedo. The Governor brushed aside some letters from Mrs. Pike and courteously told Pike to keep them. The others would be retained for further study. Meanwhile, Pike would please write a short report of his trip.

Pike would be quartered with Lieutenant Walker, said Salcedo, so that he would "be better accommodated by having a person [with him] who spoke the English language," but Pike suspected the arrangement had been made so that Walker could "act as a spy on our actions, and on those who visited us."

By mistake, Dr. Robinson was brought in ahead of schedule. During Pike's audience with the Governor, the doctor had been "standing in the guard room, boiling with indignation at being so long detained there, subject to the observations of the soldiery and gaping curiosity of the vulgar." Obviously annoyed, Salcedo asked who he was.

"A doctor who accompanied the expedition," Melgares replied.

"Let him retire," said Salcedo, and Robinson was hustled back to the guard room.

"You will dine with me," the Governor told Pike, and the conference ended.

In the account of his journey that he prepared for Salcedo, Pike stuck to the story he had told Alencaster in Santa Fe: that he had thought the Rio Grande was the Red River. Walker translated the statement into Spanish.

Salcedo himself was busy getting off dispatches, and they left no doubts of his conviction that Pike and Robinson were spies for Wilkinson, as well as unmitigated liars.

An examination of Pike's papers, he wrote to Yrujo, who was the Spanish minister in Washington, revealed "the pretext under which General Wilkinson sought to hide the real purpose of the . . . expedition. . . ." and that Wilkinson, "having decided to advance as far as the settlements of New Mexico, provided the excuses to be used so as to avoid being charged with having done so intentionally, in case he [Pike] was discovered: that Dr. Robinson, so as to acquire more knowledge, went into the Capital of the Province itself, under the pretext of looking for a Frenchman who owed him money; that Paike denied that that person belonged to his party; and finally that in everything about the said officer gave information—both by word of mouth and in writing—he has contradicted himself, not telling the truth about anything.

"As Your Excellency is well aware of the ambitious motives of the United States in conducting such expeditions; you have made representations against them to their Government . . . I send Your Excellency all the above mentioned materials so that on the basis of them Your Excellency may proceed as you judge most suitable to the service of His Majesty. . . ." Pike, thought Salcedo, "will continue to lie and will try to astonish his own Government. . . ." Salcedo was no less perspicacious than he was cautious and suspicious. Pike *would* continue to lie, not only to the Spanish but also to his superiors, including the President of the United States, in Washington.

In a letter to General Wilkinson (once Number 13 on the roster of Spanish secret agents), Salcedo said bluntly that the General was "not ignorant" of the representations made by the highest Spanish officials to the United States regarding expeditions to Spanish territory, and the General "must therefore, without any further observations or remarks on my part, be satisfied, that an offence of magnitude had been committed against his majesty, and that every individual of this party [Pike's] ought to have been considered as prisoners on the very spot. . . ." But Salcedo did not close the door forever on Wilkinson. The General might still be of some use as a spy in the American Army, and he ended his letter with the declaration that he was "without reserve," Wilkinson's "most obedient, humble, and respectful and faithful servant. . . ."

To Alencaster, Salcedo sent a message expressing the opinion that "the correspondence that was found on them [Pike and Robinson], their notes and even their own manner of speaking make it possible to believe that they have qualities which their Government thought sufficient to entrust this expedition to them, and this in itself makes one very dubious of whatever information they give."

Alencaster had been deeply disturbed by information given to him by Private Sparks (of the frozen feet), who had finally arrived in Santa Fe. Spark's intelligence, he wrote Salcedo, was to the effect that Pike had expected to rendezvous with "a considerable party of Anglo-American soldiers" on the Red River.

Alencaster also had discovered that while Pike and Robinson were in Santa Fe and other places, they had asked significant questions of various persons. One of these persons was an American tailor, Nicolas Cole, but nothing else is known of him, who had taken up residence in the New Mexico capitol. Pike and/or Robinson had asked him "what sort of people these natives were with arms, whether they were content with the government, and if they would be capable of fighting with the Anglo-Americans. . . ." The American spies also had revealed to the tailor, said Alencaster, "that in time of war with Spain or England, General Wilkinson, in agreement with the Royalists or English Government had forty thousand men ready to enter these Internal [Spanish] Provinces in order to conquer them . . . painting the said General as full of ambition for being a conqueror."

If the tailor's assertions were true, and there was no evidence that cast a shadow on them, only one conclusion can be drawn: Pike and Robinson were seeking information that would have aided the filibustering scheme of Burr and Wilkinson.

Both Salcedo and Alencaster would be severely criticized by the Spanish Foreign Office for sending Pike through the interior of the provinces and for not throwing him into jail. By this action they gave Pike an opportunity to observe the country, Spanish defences, and the general economy, as well as to talk with persons wherever he went and to disseminate propaganda injurious to the Spanish administration.

In Chihuahua, Pike enjoyed almost complete freedom, dined frequently with Salcedo, and was entertained almost daily in the homes of churchmen, officers, and civil executives. If his own account may be believed, he became a gay blade, reveling in the company of a "large collection of ladies, amongst who were two of the most celebrated in the capital. . . . the only two ladies who had spirit sufficient, and their husbands generosity enough[,] to allow them to think themselves rational beings . . . they were consequently the envy of the ladies, and the subject of scandal to prudes; their houses were the rendezvous of all the fashionable male society . . . We, as unfortunate strangers, were consequently not forgotten."

Without bashfulness, Pike demanded of Salcedo $1,000 to defray his expenses. Buying wines and good food and clothing cost money, and he could not afford to be remiss in repaying social obligations. He promised that the sum would be returned promptly by the American government. Salcedo gave him the money, asking only that Pike sign vouchers for it. And this generosity also brought the wrath of the foreign office down on Salcedo's head.

On April 9, Pike had a tearful meeting with an American, David Fero, Jr., a former soldier who had at one time been his father's ensign. Fero had resigned from the Army in 1799. There were reasons why he had to slip into Chihuahua at night and meet secretly with Pike. He had been one of Nolan's raiders, and had been captured in the fight in which Nolan had been killed. The Spanish had never permitted him to return to the United States. Pike was deeply moved by Fero's story, as he felt that Fero "possessed a brave soul, and had withstood every oppression . . . [Fero was then confined in the adjacent village of San Geronimo] Although his leaving the place . . . with the knowledge of the general [Salcedo], was in some measure clandestine, yet, a countryman, an acquaintance, and formerly a brother soldier, in a strange land, in distress, had ventured much to see me—could I deny him the interview from any motives of delicacy? No; forbid it humanity! forbid it every sentiment of my soul!"

But there were also some other emotions influencing Pike's thinking. He was aware of Wilkinson's close association with Nolan. The meeting with Fero may have been "affecting, tears standing in his eyes," but he also was anxious to help the prisoners who had operated as raiders, spies, and thieves for his beloved commander. Wilkinson would be grateful to him.

He gave Fero some money, sent him off in the night, and wrote an impassioned appeal to Salcedo in behalf of all Nolan's men still held in Mexico. Pike conceded that Nolan's gang had entered "the territories of his catholic majesty in a clandestine manner, equally in violation of the treaties between the two governments . . . [and] could not be reclaimed or noticed by their country. . . ." He declared that "from every information I have received on the subject, the men on the party were innocent, believing that Nolan had passports from the Spanish governor to carry on the traffic of horses. . . ." He begged Salcedo "to inform me if any thing can be done towards restoring these poor fellows to their liberty, friends and country, and in a particular manner I intercede for Fero." Salcedo was not stirred enough by the appeal to recommend clemency for the prisoners.

Now Dr. Robinson began to play a hand that con-

"My intentions," he told Salcedo, "were not to accompany the said expedition except to the point which was considered closest to the most Northerly of the Towns of New Mexico, where I had to attend to some pecuniary tained cards he had concealed in his sleeve. He pretended to turn against Wilkinson, Pike, and his country.
matters, and also having a lively desire to know the Country, for the sake of knowing whether it were more suitable for a man of my profession than the one in which I lived.

" . . . I take note of the fact that I am not involved with the purposes of the above-mentioned expedition, directly or indirectly; I had not confessed to accompanying a military expedition, because my spirit rebelled at the idea of being a traitor to a friend from whom I had received many favors and who merited my gratitude and not my ill will.

"It is also true that General Wilkinson did not know of my intentions to visit this Country because perhaps he would not have permitted it.

"Finally, it is my desire to be a subject of His Catholic Majesty, and in such case I have a plan to set forth for your Consideration and Sponsorship, and in the meantime I am, with the greatest respect your most obedient and humble servant."

Perplexed, Salcedo did not reply. He could ask himself any number of questions, but arrive at no satisfactory answers. He bided his time, keeping silent, and waiting for some development that would explain the mystery of the doctor's proposal. And it came a few days later.

Juan Pedro Walker translated a second note the doctor sent to the Governor. Robinson now proposed that he be sent on an exploring expedition, as a subject of His Catholic Majesty, to the disputed areas of Louisiana, as a "knowledge of that Country, most especially in this Period, appears to be of extreme interest to the Court of Spain, because of the claims which the English and Americans—Congress of the United States—are sustaining. . . ." Robinson assured Salcedo that he was "well acquainted with the plan and intention of United States and Great Britain about this matter. . . ."

Salcedo had no difficulty believing him. An American spy would be expected to know the plan and intention of his country. But that did not mean Robinson would become a defector and could be trusted.

Robinson sought to convince Salcedo of his sincerity with the assertion that he personally had presented a proposal to the "Congress of the United States, to colonize a part of that Country which is along the Western Ocean to about 45 degrees of Northern latitude," and that he had received congressional "approval and sponsorship." But since that time, Robinson had changed his mind because of his "knowledge of the Geographical Situation of the Country, and an even better knowledge of the rights of the Court of Spain," and he believed "that the claims of the United States and Great Britain will be, exactly and eventually, proved useless." Secrecy about the matter was necessary, said Robinson, and he did "not wish that my friend Lieutenant Pike nor any American know of the cause of my detention, for various reasons: 1st, So that the expedition [which he wished to lead for Spain] may not be known to any foreign Power; 2nd, So as to avoid the confiscation of my possessions in the United States—

which would be the case if it were known that I was remaining here voluntarily. . . ."

Salcedo had no more trouble reaching a decision about the doctor's scheme. He had no intention of being held responsible for permitting an American spy to become a subject of His Catholic Majesty, but above all he would not be stupid enough to give a defector command of an expedition and have it delivered lock, stock, and burro, into American hands as an invading force. Whatever happened to Pike would also be the fate of Robinson.

It was a wise decision. For Robinson's real motive would come to light in a dispatch to Salcedo from Alencaster in Santa Fe.

Salcedo had sent Alencaster urgent orders to be on the alert for more Americans, to send out parties to scout for them, and, if necessary, to repel them with force. Alencaster had obeyed, and had made preparations to defend his jurisdiction. But it would not be against American invaders only that he would be obliged to defend it. He was facing a possible revolt of his own people. And he wrote Salcedo "a sad observation" that he had received "very highly surreptitious information and had overheard the conversations of the people about whether the Anglo-Americans will come and the possibility that they may make themselves master of this Province, without observing any displeasure among these people or hearing them express animosity or willingness to risk their lives to guard their Homes; and they speak with the greatest insipidity and timidity—which indications are very dangerous to us, and I can envision myself in the situation of having to struggle to prevent the horrible results. . . ."

The people of New Mexico were ready to welcome

the Americans and would not oppose them. And Alencaster had information that such an invasion was in the making. It had come to him from Private Sparks, who said that a force of American soldiers had been sent out to meet Pike. Then the expatriate tailor, Nicholas Cole, had sworn that Pike and Robinson had told him an army of 40,000 men were ready to march on the internal Spanish provinces. Then had come additional alarming intelligence from another member of Pike's company, Private Daugherty, who had stated that when Pike had started for the Spanish frontier, he had been informed by General Wilkinson that if he had not returned by Christmas it would be presumed he had been taken prisoner by the Spanish. And Daugherty had more to reveal: Wilkinson also had told Pike not to worry, that forces would be sent out to rescue him, columns containing "three to four thousand men each, that they would go along the principal Rivers, and that he [Daugherty] thought it beyond doubt that those parties would now be near."

Alencaster begged Salcedo for more dragoons and arms with which to save New Mexico.

Robinson, a shrewd observer, had noted the dissension and unrest in New Mexico, the hatred of the natives for the cruel and fanatical domination by the priests, to whom military and civil authorities gave every support. Robinson believed the stage was set for a revolt that would open the gates to Burr and Wilkinson, and he wanted to remain to help incite the uprising. Robinson did not know then that not only had the conspiracy of Burr and Wilkinson been exposed but Burr had been charged with treason and Wilkinson had informed on Burr and would be the main witness against him.

But Robinson soon would be thankful that he had not been granted sanctuary by Salcedo, for distressing rumors began to reach Chihuahua. Burr had been arrested and would be tried. And General Wilkinson had been accused of conspiring with him to invade the Spanish dominions.

Neither Pike nor Robinson would know any factual details of what Pike termed the "convulsions" in the Mississippi Valley, but they would hear enough to give them some sleepless hours. And in time, they would learn that Wilkinson had exposed Burr in letters to President Jefferson, describing himself as being "staggered" by the immensity of the plot and his "discovery" of it. The General told the President that Burr planned to raise a force of 10,000 men, rendezvous in New Orleans, and from there attack Vera Cruz. Having achieved at least a tentative peace with Spanish forces on the Texas frontier, Wilkinson was prepared to defend New Orleans to the death against the despicable disloyalty of the former Vice-President.

Wilkinson, of course, would not have to defend anything. He had made a highly suspicious deal with the Spanish that had established a kind of no-man's-land between their lines in Texas. His main problem would be to conceal his own dishonorable plotting with Burr. And in that, as usual, he would be successful.

Pike and Robinson would know all these things in time, but for months, while their concerns mounted (and especially those of Pike), they would wonder how they themselves would fare once the cards fell into place on the legal table.

Wilkinson himself would give Pike a warning about

this phase of the nasty situation. The General had received Governor Salcedo's letter, which told him for the first time that Pike was alive, and he had written Pike: "After having counted you among the dead, I was most agreeably surprised to find . . . that you were in his possession. . . ." And Wilkinson did not overlook the chance to add a few words in his own favor by regretting that Pike "had missed the object of your enterprise" by failing to find the Red River.

Nor did Wilkinson neglect to apprise Pike that he would "hear of the scenes in which I have been engaged, and may be informed that the traitors whose infamous designs against the constitution and government of our country *I have detected, exposed, and destroyed*, are vainly attempting to explain their conduct by inculpating me; and, among other devices, they have asserted that your's and lieutenant Wilkinson's enterprise was a *premeditated co-operation with Burr*." Wilkinson told Pike that he was "on the wing for Richmond, in Virginia, to confront the arch traitor and his host of advocates," and in his haste he did not have the "leisure to commune with you as amply as I could desire. . . ."

Now Wilkinson made the point toward which he had been working. Pike "*must be cautious, extremely cautious how you breathe a word*, because the publicity may excite a spirit of adventure adverse to the interests of our government, or injurious to the maturation of those plans, which may hereafter be found necessary and justifiable by the government . . . if you possess in your information aught which you may desire to communicate in person, you are at liberty to proceed, by the shortest route, to the seat of government [Washington], near which you will find me, if alive . . . I pray you to *attend particularly to the injunctions* of this hasty letter, and to believe me, whilst I am your general, Your friend."

Pike would not receive the General's communication until he was freed, and then he would write him: "We had heard in the Spanish dominions of the convulsions of the western country, originating in Mr. Burr's plans, and that you were implicated; sometimes that you were arrested, sometimes superceded, &c. Those reports—although I never gave credit to them—gave me great unhappiness, as I conceived that the shafts of columny were aiming at your fame and honor, where they had hitherto stood high, and were revered and respected by every class . . . I hope ere long will the villany be unmasked and malignity and slander hide their heads."

One day late in April, Pike and Robinson picked up a piece of gossip that mystified them. It was that "an American officer had gone on to the city of Mexico." This was somewhat of an "enigma" because they "conceived that the jealousy of the Spanish government would have prevented any foreign officer from penetrating the country. . . ." The officer was "Mr. Burling, a citizen of Mississippi Territory. . . ."

What Pike and Robinson had no way of knowing was that General Wilkinson was up to his old tricks. Walter Burling, of Natchez, had been an aide to Wilkinson at the time the Spanish and American forces faced each other on the Sabine River in 1806. An open clash had been averted largely through Wilkinson's clandestine negotiations with the Spanish commander.

Wilkinson saw himself in a position to make a killing. He planned a scheme in a manner that would not bring reflections on him should it be exposed. His first move was to induce Burling to ask him to be sent to Mexico to purchase mules. Then he officially approved Burling's request. But Burling was not only to be a mule buyer; he was also to be a spy and a private emissary for Wilkinson. As a secret agent, Burling was "to avail" himself "of the present alarm, produced by Col. Burr's project." And Burling was to travel "by the interior and return by water, in order to examine both routes, relative to their practicability and the means of defence the Spanish possess. . . ."

This appeared to be a proper spying mission that might be valuable to the United States. But while Burling was performing it, he was (unknown to Washington or the Army) to take a letter from Wilkinson to the Viceroy in Mexico City. The letter would explain to the Spanish government how Wilkinson alone had prevented the invasion of Mexico planned by Burr and had saved Mexico from a costly war with the United States. For this service, Wilkinson demanded no less than $100,000, cash.

Burling would get neither mules nor money, and his spying would be wasted effort.

In Chihuahua, Pike made a final attempt to recover all his papers. Salcedo refused to release them. Not only were Pike and Robinson military spies, said the Governor, but they were guilty of attempts to foment a civil rebellion in New Mexico, and they could rest assured that their conduct "will be represented in no very favorable point of view" to the American government.

Salcedo had had all he wanted of Pike and his company, and on April 27, he told them to prepare to depart the following day for Nagodoches and the United

States border. Pike would please take his two grizzly bears and his other souvenirs with him. His men who had not yet arrived from the North would be sent home in due time.

Salcedo's orders to the military personnel who would escort "the foreigners" made it clear that they were to be prevented "throughout the journey from taking notes, sketching maps, or departing from the route which the whole party is taking." Even Pike's watch was to be taken from him.

It was Pike's old friend, Melgares, who led the party out of Chihuahua on the afternoon of April 28. Various other officers took command of the escort during the next sixty-three days as the company plodded slowly over the vast deserts, mountains, and plains of northern Mexico and Texas, through the Sierra Madre Oriental, across the Rio Grande, to San Antonio, across the Colorado and the Brazos, through Nagodoches, and across the Sabine.

At four o'clock on the afternoon of July 1, Natchitoches was reached, and Pike could not find language to "express the gaity of my heart, when I once more beheld the standard of my country waved aloft!

"All hail! cried I, the ever sacred name of country, in which is embraced that of kindred friends, and every other tie which is dear to the soul of man!"

Orders from Wilkinson were waiting for him.

25

PIKE WAS ILL IN NATCHITOCHES, and he had difficulty with his vision. Wilkinson had ordered him to proceed to Washington, and he had planned to ascend the Mississippi to St. Louis for a reunion with his family, then travel to Pittsburgh by way of the Ohio, and go on from there to the Capital. But he was physically unable to start at once on the long, circuitous journey, and Mrs. Pike and their daughter, Clarissa, hurried down the Mississippi to join him. It was then Pike learned that a son born to his wife shortly after his departure for the West had died in infancy.

Although he knew extreme exhaustion, he struggled to prepare his journal for publication and to repudiate the charges made by newspapers that he was involved in the Burr-Wilkinson conspiracy.

He was admittedly proud of his work as a spy against

the Spanish, and he wrote Wilkinson: "From our un-remitting attention day and night, the immense territory they led us through, the long time we were in their country, I have been able to collect—I make bold to assert —a correct account of their military force, regular and irregular; also, important and interesting information on geographical situations, political sentiments, and disposi-tions of the people of every class, manners, arts, re-sources, riches, revenues, value and production of their mines, situation, &c. &c. . . . By the serjeant [Meek] who is still in the rear . . . I expect many other communica-tions of importance from many individuals, who promised to forward them by him."

He might have mentioned how valuable Dr. Robin-son had been to him as his colleague in espionage, but that thought apparently did not occur to him.

As for Meek, he would not arrive. He had killed Private Miller in a drunken fight and had been impris-oned by the Spanish, not to be released until 1820 to return to the United States.

"From the foregoing statement," Pike continued to Wilkinson, "your excellency will observe that I yet possess immense matter . . . But my papers are in a mutilated state, from the absolute necessity I was under to write on small pieces in the Spanish country; also, from being injured in the gun barrels, some of which I filed three times off to take out the papers."

Pike assured Wilkinson that he had commanded his men not to talk at all about the expedition, for in their "breasts lay the whole secret of my papers . . . I have charged them as to communications, and shall dispose of them in such a manner as not to put it in their power to give things much publicity."

The animosity of numerous southern editors for Wilkinson was extended to Pike, who now wore a captain's bars but who revealed a feeling of bitterness because a grateful country had not hailed him as a returning hero, and a resentfulness against the War Department because he had not been promoted to a colonelcy and given command of a regiment.

Newspapers thundered that he was "a parasite of Wilkinson," and undeserving of honors. One Natchez weekly was particularly virulent in its editorial assaults upon him; the paper would continue them for two years and would charge that he was one of Wilkinson's dupes "who pretend not to credit the charges which have been exhibited against him. It can only be a pretense—a person might as well deny the light of the sun, as to deny the truths which are well known."

Even his aging father, Major Zebulon Pike, held some suspicions about the activities of his son, writing Secretary Dearborn to ask if he had received orders from the "Government on His late exploring expedition, from the President, Yourself, or Genl. Wilkinson, and if any or how late the last information or communication from him . . . the anxiety and concern, exhibited for his safety, by an affectionate Mother and Wife, is Great. . . ."

Pike already had reached Natchitoches when his father wrote to the Secretary. On the face of the elder Pike's letter, Dearborn scribbled: "Tell him his son is safe. . . ."

Pike finally wrote to his father in August from Natchitoches that he soon would leave for Washington.

And he wrote to him again from New Orleans in September as he was preparing to sail. In his second letter, he revealed his growing anger at the failure of the War Department to promote him. He believed he should have received his captaincy a year sooner than it had been approved, which would have put him in line for a majority even before his return from the West. And he threatened that if he did not receive it soon, he would quit the Army and take his family to live among the western savages. [The promotion would not come until the spring of 1808, but during the next four years Pike would rise comparatively rapidly in rank, and he would be a general when he died.]

Pike's craving for recognition and plaudits such as those received by Lewis and Clark got out of hand and became an obsession. He felt that he had made immense sacrifices to serve his country, and he wanted an immediate reward. The criticism and castigations leveled at him by newspapers and political opponents of Burr and Wilkinson were, to his way of thinking, base slanders that the government he had served so devotedly and unselfishly should bring to a quick halt.

Soon after his arrival in Washington, he petitioned for the command of a corps of the new and larger Army that Congress was preparing to authorize. Secretary Dearborn did not give it to him. A lot of feeling against Pike existed on Capital Hill, engendered by his known closeness to General Wilkinson, and Dearborn did not relish tangling with Congress over the matter. But Dearborn offered Pike the rank of major in the Rifle Corps, and ordered him transferred back to the Mississippi Valley—

after his duties and obligations, such as finishing his reports, were completed.

Pike was both incensed and deeply hurt, for the assignment meant that he would serve under some general who was "heavy, dull, fat, unenterprising and incapable." And even worse, he would have over him some lieutenant-colonel who "would doubtless be some rough back-woods Indian fighter with no ideas of organization or discipline." These men "would reap all the honor."

Once more he appealed to the Secretary to make him at least a lieutenant-colonel, but Dearborn did not reply. Frustrated and furious, Pike did not give up his campaign to have the spotlight of fame turned on him. He worked feverishly to complete his journal, seeing it as the instrument which would give him equal stature with the detested Lewis and Clark. The work was completed shortly after the end of 1807.

Pike blamed the delay in submitting it to the War Department on General Wilkinson, who had usurped much of his time "since my arrival at the seat of Government." He could not blame the General for the poor quality or the incompleteness of his production, but he attributed those deficiencies to the Spanish who had confiscated his documents and to the adverse conditions and terrible ordeals under which he had made the western journey. He also defended himself on the ground that he did not possess the talents or "passions for the Botanist or Mineralogists. . . ." but declared that had he possessed them, he could have done no better because of the "various duties I was obliged to perform of commanding Officer, Surveyor; Astronomer; hunter; and advanced guard, together with the dreary season in which we travelled part of the route; with our minds much more actively employed in forming resources for our preservation from famine; and defence against any savage enemy who might assail us, than examining the productions of Nature . . . Instead of our eyes being directed to the Ground; they were endeavoring to pearce the Wild before us—giving distinction and form to moveing Bodies on the distant Prairies—or enjoying the Rapturous sublimity of the unbounded prospects. . . ."

When he received Pike's reports, Dearborn merely sent them on to the President with a note saying that Pike's "map of the Country through which he passed will soon be completed." Some of Pike's maps were drawn by a draftsman working under his direction, but the map of the Spanish provinces was of dubious origin. Mr. Jefferson would be out of office when he would receive a letter from the famous scientist and explorer, Alexander von Humboldt, which stated bluntly that Pike had stolen his map of New Spain [Mexico and the Southwest], "and had taken, rather ungraciously, my report which he undoubtedly obtained in Washington with the copy of this map, and besides, he has also extracted from it all the names. I am sorry over my cause for complaint about a citizen of the United States who otherwise showed such fine courage. I don't find my name in his book and a quick glance at Mr. Pike's map may prove to you from where he got it."

Mr. Jefferson expressed his regrets. But as a former President he had no authority to take any official action, and Pike had died at the time Mr. Jefferson wrote to Humboldt. He felt that whatever Pike did "was on a principle of enlarging knolege and not for filthy shillings and pence . . . I am sorry he omitted even to acknoledge

the source of his information. It has been an oversight
. . . Let me solicit your forgiveness then of a declared
hero, of an honest and zealous patriot, who lived and died
for his country."

In his desperate efforts to improve his own station
and obtain the emoluments he thought he deserved, Pike
went over the heads of General Wilkinson and Secretary
Dearborn and sought to endear himself to President
Jefferson with letters and gifts sent directly to the White
House. He had been in Washington only a few days when
he wrote Mr. Jefferson that he had sent "by the bearer a
small Box containing Pecans [brought from Mississippi]
. . . also a Box and quiver of arrows which are the
offensive weapons of the Appache's . . . There was
shipped from New Orleans for your Excelly. in the Brig
Neptune Capt. Shepheard Master, bound to Baltimore a
pair of Grisly Bears—mail and femail—which I brought
from the dividing ridges, of the Pacific, and Atlantic
Oceans . . . and are considered by the natives of that
country as the most ferocious Animals of the Continent
. . ."

The President was delighted and wrote to thank Pike
for the bows and arrows and the cubs, but he did not
mention the pecans. It was Mr. Jefferson's opinion that
the bears would be a valuable contribution to a museum
maintained by the noted scholar of natural history,
Charles Willson Peale, in Philadelphia.

Peale also was delighted to have the cubs, and told
Mr. Jefferson he thought there was "a good chance of
their giving produce."

The bears gave no produce of their kind, but they did
raise continual hell and attacked any person or beast who

approached their cages. One of them succeeded in breaking out, terrified the community, and concealed itself in the cellar of Philosophical Hall. Peale shot it. He then killed the other, and had both mounted. Alive and dead, the bears were labeled as a gift from President Jefferson. Peale made no mention of Pike.

Burr's acquittal in Richmond in the fall of 1807 had alleviated to some extent the stigma which the public had attached to Pike, but it did not entirely terminate the antagonism for him which had existed in the Congress even before his return from the West.

When it was proposed that Pike and his men receive extra compensation for their explorations, Congressman John Rowan of Kentucky, an arch enemy of both Burr and Wilkinson, took the floor to remark that he had "received a letter from Orleans that a Mr. Joseph Ballenger [Sergeant Ballinger, who descended the Arkansas with Lieutenant Wilkinson], a friend of Burr, had returned from an expedition with Captain Pike, and was incensed at Wilkinson for blowing up the [Burr] expedition, as he had engaged two or three nations of Indians to join Colonel Burr."

Representative Rowan informed his colleagues that he had " . . . since spoken to Colonel Ballenger, a brother of this person, [John Ballinger of Kentucky] who informed me that his brother had been sent by Wilkinson for the purpose of promoting the [Burr] project. . . .

"If this is the case, and Mr. Pike is privy to this confederacy, he ought not to receive compensation."

The argument that Lewis and Clark and their men had received rewards was to no avail. The bill failed not because members of Congress felt that the men Pike had called "a dam'd set of rascals" deserved the description and not because they were deemed unworthy of being given more than their regular Army pay. It failed because too many persons in high positions in Washington believed that Pike had conspired with Burr and Wilkinson and that he had made his western journey chiefly in connection with their treasonous schemes. And the fact that both Burr and Wilkinson and been acquitted of such charges did not weaken this conviction.

Pike, seething with anger, took the case to both the War Department and the newspapers. "I understand," he wrote the *National Intelligencer*, "that the hon. John Rowan . . . mentioned that he had been informed that a certain Joseph Ballenger who accompanied me in part of my tour . . . was employed as an emissary of Col. Burr at the instigation of Gen. Wilkinson, to seduce the Indians to join in the scheme of Col. Burr to attack the Spanish provinces. . . ." During the time Ballinger had been with him, Pike said, "he never directly—or indirectly, insinuated his having any commission from General Wilkinson —and that I am conscious he had no opportunity, and did not make use of any intrigue, or in fact hold any conference with the Indians more than any other private individual of the party."

Pike was neither saying all he might have said nor telling all he knew. He knew that Ballinger had been for years an operator for Wilkinson in the General's intrigues with the Spanish. He knew Wilkinson had ordered that Ballinger be taken on the expedition, not only as a confidential agent for Wilkinson but as a bodyguard for the General's son. And Pike knew that he had falsified Ballinger's enlistment record and had elevated him immediately to a sergeancy over veteran corporals and privates who fully merited promotion. And Pike knew that Ballinger had been with him *only* as far as the Great Bend of the Arkansas. But Pike did *not* know whether Ballinger had conferences with Indian leaders south of that point.

From Rowan's remarks, Pike wrote Dearborn, " . . . a tacit inference might be drawn that my late Tour was . . . connected with the nefarious plans of Aaron Burr and his associates . . . I feel it a duty to myself; my family; and my profession; to request of you a testimonial which may shut the mouth of Calumny—and strike dumb the voice of slander. I have therefore to request of you Sir to Honor me with a communication which may be calculated to present to the Speaker of the House of Representatives . . . and that I may have permission to give publicity to the letter. . . ."

Dearborn, obviously anxious to have the noise quelled, immediately came to Pike's defense, writing him: "I can with pleasure observe that altho' the two exploring expeditions you have performed were not previously ordered by the President . . . there were frequent communications on the subject of each, between Genl. Wilkinson & this Department, of which the President . . . was acquainted from time to time, and it will be no more than what justice requires, to say that your conduct in each of those expeditions met the approbation of the President and that the Information you obtained and communicated to the Executive . . . has been considered as highly interesting in a political, geographical, & historical view. And you may rest assured that your services are held in high estimation by the President . . . and if any opinion of my own can afford you any satisfaction, I can very frankly declare that I consider the public much indebted to you. . . ."

Pike was deeply grateful, and sent to Dearborn and the President "the effusions of a Heart impress'd . . . for the very honorable testimonial. . . ."

Now he felt that he had reason to believe he had been victorious in the fight to defend his honor and had successfully repudiated the accusation that he was a tool of Wilkinson and Burr in the aborted conspiracy. But it was only a dream that would never come true. He would never escape completely from the shadow which had been cast upon him by the traitors.

The esteem in which the Presidents (Jefferson and his successor, Madison) held Pike brought him few if any special favors. Neither of them interfered in the course of his military life as it was decreed by the War Department in the years 1808 and 1809. He was sent back to his old station, Cantonment Bellfontaine, at St. Louis, where as a major, he commanded a small detachment. Then followed a brief tour of duty at Fort McHenry, in Maryland, after which he was transferred once more to the western frontier, serving at various stations in the South.

Once again, he was on the Wilkinson's staff. The General had been sent West to prepare defenses for the vital Mississippi delta region. With his incredible good luck and his inexplicable political influence, Wilkinson had succeeded in washing off some of the mud thrown upon him by the Burr trial. Powerful members of Congress had demanded that his conduct be investigated, but President Jefferson and Secretary Dearborn had been able to prevent a public hearing by convening a military court of inquiry to hear the charges against the controversial and troublesome General.

The three members appointed to sit on the court were not only close friends of Wilkinson but also his subordinates. In the regular course of Army business, they would be subject to his orders. They gave him a clean bill of health, which included an acquittal on the charge that he had been a paid secret agent for the Spanish.

Wilkinson lost no time resuming his dishonest career. En route from Baltimore to New Orleans, he arranged to have his ship stop in Havana so that he could sell (in violation of the American embargo then existing against such commerce) a large quantity of goods he had bought in the United States. The merchandise was transported to Cuba at the government's expense.

In New Orleans, Wilkinson established a system of graft that would have done credit to Tammany Hall's most corrupt politicians. While he was in command there, hundreds of soldiers died of malnutrition, fever, disease, and from eating moldy flour and meat that contained maggots. He refused to obey an order from Secretary of War William Eustis, who had succeeded Dearborn, to move his camp up the Mississippi to the higher ground and better climate of Fort Adams. Instead, he moved it lower on the river to a location which the *Natchez Chronicle* called "one of the foulest swamps on the banks of the Mississippi." But Wilkinson did not propose to be separated from his lucrative stealing in New Orleans.

Meanwhile, he had once more arranged to have an agent sent to Mexico City. His pretext for the War Department record was that pressure should be brought on the Spanish government to release Pike's men who were still being held in Chihuahua. But he also told Dearborn he had heard that Spain was moving troops toward the Missouri River, and he voiced the fear that Great Britain would be able to establish a foothold in Mexico that would disrupt American commerce.

As he had done so many times before, Dearborn swallowed the bait, and authorized Wilkinson to select the man for the assignment. Wilkinson selected one of his aides, Captain Daniel Hughes, who had long been in his confidence. In Hughes's pocket went a letter from Wilkinson to General Simon de Herrara of the Spanish army. It asked for a testimonial to the effect that Wilkinson had never made any secret agreements with Herrara, who had commanded the Spanish forces that faced the Americans on the Sabine. Wilkinson had been publicly accused of selling out to Herrara by establishing a "neutral zone" along the disputed border. And Hughes was given another private job to do for Wilkinson. It was to obtain a large number of horses that could be sold in the United States.

Hughes proved himself to be a competent agent. He delivered Wilkinson's letter to Herrara, obtained the release of Pike's men (with the exception of Sergeant Meek, who was detained for the murder of Private Miller), and when he recrossed the border to the United States, he brought with him a large herd of horses.

The General's malfeasance and venality once again brought Pike into disrepute. The Major was his confidant, and Wilkinson favored him over officers senior to him. Cried the *Chronicle:* "An old and respected officer has had his command wrested from him, to give it to a . . . parasite of Wilkinson," and to "prop up the rotten fame of the Commander in Chief."

[230]

Wilkinson appointed Pike temporary Military Agent, a high and responsible post, but Secretary Eustis, fully aware of Pike's unpopularity, refused to give him permanent status.

Between seven and eight hundred soldiers died in the filthy camp that Wilkinson maintained until he was summarily removed and the command given to General Wade Hampton. Hampton immediately transferred Pike to Natchez.

"How are the Mighty Fallen," said an article in the *Chronicle*, " . . . and thus disappointed the gold prospect of General Wilkinson's pet bully, the knight of Santa Fe . . . This rebuff . . . will fill the junior major with philosophy to meet an investigation of his trip to Santa Fe. . . ."

Wilkinson was ordered to appear before a court-martial on charges of corruption and neglect of his duties and responsibilities. Wilkinson's plea was that he was a persecuted martyr and that every action of his had been taken with the thought of "tender care for his men." He asked that Pike be summoned as one of his defense witnesses, but red tape initiated by Secretary Eustis and General Hampton kept Pike on duty.

However, as far as Pike was concerned, Wilkinson was prepared to meet such an exigency. Actually, two years before, as if he had fully expected that Pike would be kept from testifying in his behalf when the chips were down, he had prepared to meet the situation. He had obtained from Pike a lengthy statement which pictured him as a man of unsullied honor, unquestionable integrity, and an officer who had never in his long career deviated from performing the duties given him. The statement was in the form of a sworn deposition in which Pike had answered eleven questions, which had been prepared by Wilkinson himself.

Pike testified: "I have never known general Wilkinson to neglect a point of duty, nor by word or deed, to injure the service of his country.

"I do most sincerely believe that general Wilkinson has, to the best of his judgement, and utmost zeal, pursued the interest, honor and safety of his country.

"General Wilkinson never did propose to me any plan, project or design, which I conceived unjust, or of such a nature as was injurious to those who administered the government of our country, or which was in violation of its constitution. . . .

"I received the first idea or intimation of the plans of Aaron Burr and his associates, through the medium of the Mexican gazette, printed at the City of Mexico, in the Spanish language, which I met with at the post of Chihuahua . . . in March, 1807.

"To the best of my recollection, general Wilkinson never mentioned the name of colonel Burr to me, previous to my meeting him at Washington, in October, 1807, except on Burr's halt at [Fort] Massac, when on his way down the river Ohio, in June, 1805. He then spoke to me of him as the late Vice President; a man of talents; and particularly of his valedictory address to the Senate of the United States."

But Wilkinson did not need Pike's contrived deposition. He was acquitted by the court-martial. One of the officers who sat in judgment of him also had served on the previous court of inquiry, by which he had been found not guilty.

26

LATE IN APRIL, 1813, Brigadier-General Pike wrote a short letter to his father, Major Pike. It said: "I embark tomorrow in the fleet at Sackett's Harbor, [an important naval base in the War of 1812, in New York State at the eastern end of Lake Ontario] at the head of a column of 1,500 choice troops, on a secret expedition. If success attends my steps, honor and glory await my name—if defeat, still shall it be said we died like brave men, and conferred honor, even in death, on the AMERICAN NAME.

"Should I be the happy mortal destined to turn the scale of war, will you not rejoice, O my father? May Heaven be propitious, and smile on the cause of my country. But if we are destined to fall, may my fall be like Wolfe's—to sleep in the arms of victory."

It was the last letter of his life.

The "secret expedition" was to attack and destroy the defenses of York (Toronto). Pike would be in command of a brigade.

A fleet of fourteen armed American transports appeared off York on the morning of April 27. The landing was sharply resisted by rifle fire and shore batteries. For a time, Pike observed the fighting from shipboard, but at last he told his aides: "By God, I can't stay here any longer. Come on, jump into my boat."

Thereafter, Pike directed the assault on land. Casualties were heavy on both sides, but the Americans moved forward steadily, and the British defenders, realizing their defeat was inevitable, ordered a retreat. As they withdrew, they deliberately fired into one of their own powder magazines, causing it to explode.

"The effect," said a report to the War Department, "was terrible. Fragments of timber, and huge stones of which the magazine walls were built, were scattered in every direction over a space of several hundred yards.

"Fifty-two Americans lay dead, and 180 were wounded. So badly had the affair been managed that 40 of the British also lost their lives by the explosion."

One of the mortally wounded was General Pike. A piece of stone had struck him in the back, fracturing his spine.

He was carried to a boat and taken out to the Flagship Madison. From his cabin he could hear cheering, and he asked the meaning of it. "Victory!" an aide told him. "The Union Jack is going down, General. The Stars and Stripes are going up!"

Pike lived for several hours suffering terrible agony. When a captured British flag was brought to him, he motioned to have it placed under his head.

A few minutes later he died.

27

FOR FIVE YEARS AFTER his return from Mexico with Pike, Dr. Robinson practised medicine in several Mississippi Valley towns, virtually unnoticed. Pike had tried to secure an Army commission for him as a captain, but the best the War Department would offer was an appointment as an ensign. Robinson would not accept such a low rank.

By some mysterious means, word got to Secretary of State Monroe in 1812 that Robinson's experience fitted him for an assignment as an American spy in Mexico. It was a mission Monroe wanted carried out. Robinson was summoned to Washington. There he saw Pike and told him that Monroe was proposing that he accept engagement as an espionage agent. Pike at once sent Monroe a letter in which he strongly recommended his old colleague. Robinson would, Pike told Monroe, " . . . be a person eminently calculated for this undertaking."

Wilkinson was apprised of the matter. He was in close touch with Pike. Both had intimate knowledge of Dr. Robinson's true sentiments, especially those regarding Spain. They were aware that Robinson had become a violent and irreconcilable revolutionist, dedicated to aiding the Mexicans to throw off the Spanish yoke. How much of this information either of them imparted to Monroe, if, indeed, they mentioned it at all, is not a matter of record. Monroe's own attitude, however, was not as secret as his plans to spy on the Spanish. Forcing Spain to relinquish its possessions in North America would have been in accord with his utmost desires. He was not, however, willing to chance becoming involved in a war with another European power to bring it about. The United States had all it could handle at the moment in a first-class war with Great Britain.

Monroe sent Robinson to Mexico with letters to high Spanish officials. The doctor was to pose as an ambassador of goodwill and to assure the Spanish government of the unqualified friendship of the United States; and he also was to spy on Spanish military defenses.

Robinson's mission was a failure, due largely to General Salcedo's refusal to be fooled. The General, now holding a position of great influence, had not forgotten that he had accused Pike and Robinson of trying to foment unrest in Mexico, and he had not changed his mind about what he believed had been their true intentions. Salcedo prevented Robinson from deceiving other Spanish officials.

But Robinson was not easily defeated, and on his way home he got in touch with revolutionary leaders. With them he plotted the invasion of Mexico with a force from the United States—the old scheme of Burr and

Wilkinson, but now with a different goal. Robinson wanted to establish a republic controlled by peons.

Back in the United States, Robinson issued inflammatory broadsides calling upon "noble, brave and enterprising" young Americans to ignore the war with England and rally with him to liberate the Mexicans, who for "three hundred years have been borne down by the yoke of cruel oppression." That was too much for Monroe at the moment, and he threatened Robinson with legal action if he did not desist.

Robinson did not stop. Instead, he intensified his campaign. Pike was dead, but he wrote that Pike "would have been with us, had he lived," and he quoted in his pamphlets an excerpt from Pike's journal, in which Pike had written, "Should an army of Americans ever march into that country [Mexico] . . . they will only have to march from province to province, and be hailed by the united forces of grateful millions as their deliverers and saviors, whilst our national character, would be resounded, to the most distant nations of the Earth."

Robinson left no doubt that he and Pike had been linked with Wilkinson, if not with Burr, in a plot to invade the Spanish provinces. And Robinson carried on the dream by himself, became a general in the Mexican revolutionary forces, and led several unsuccessful raids over the border.

But the revolution failed to develop as Robinson had hoped and had planned it. Ill, discouraged, and impecunious, he went to live in New Orleans. He would die there, disillusioned and despondent, on September 29, 1819.

28

GENERAL WILKINSON outlived both Pike and Robinson.

In 1813, he made such a miserable fiasco of the campaign against Montreal that he was removed from his command. Discredited and disgraced as a soldier, he went to live on the plantation near New Orleans that he had purchased with money obtained through his corrupt practices.

But his luck still had not run out. He received an honorable discharge from the Army. However, no post was offered him. The remarkable political influence he had enjoyed for so many years had vanished. He was ignored by every official in a position to do him a favor.

But without post or portfolio, Wilkinson still believed he could extort more money from the Spanish. He went to Mexico City and applied for a grant of land as another reward for his long service as a secret agent for Spain in the highest councils of the American Army. It was his contention that by making unauthorized deals with Spanish commanders on the Texas frontier he had saved Spain from a costly and disastrous war with the United States.

To help defray expenses in Mexico, he obtained an appointment as a representative of the American Bible Society.

The Spanish had had enough of Wilkinson. His requests were refused.

He died from smoking opium on December 28, 1825.

Bibliographical Notes

THE TRUE STORY of Pike and his relations with General Wilkinson are well known only to the comparatively small number of scholars who have studied the complex and generally dull documents pertaining to the careers of these two men. In this book, I have tried to tell the story in a way that will be interesting, as well as accurate, to anyone who enjoys the history of the early American West.

A comprehensive understanding of Pike's life and adventures cannot be gained simply from a reading of his original journals. Standing alone, the journals present only a part (actually a very small part) of the whole picture. Pike deleted material from his original writings that he thought might dull the rosy light in which he sought to bathe himself, or which he "conceived" (one of his favorite words) would reflect unfavorably on his puerile reverence for Wilkinson. He sought to protect the General and himself with asterisks.

The original journals, however, must be studied because they are the genesis of the story; but they must be placed in juxtaposition to an almost countless number of reports, documents, statements, and correspondence and must be read simultaneously with them if an accurate and complete account is to be obtained.

This has been made possible by the painstaking work of two brilliant researchers and editors, Elliott Coues and Donald Jackson. The volumes they have published, some seventy years apart, proffer to students incomparable mines of source materials.

Pike's own book was published in 1810 by C. & A. Conrad & Company of Philadelphia, which went bankrupt a short time later. Its title was:

> *An Account of Expeditions to the Sources of the Mississippi, and Through the Western Parts of Louisiana, to the Sources of the Arkansas, Kans, La Platte, and Pierre Juan, Rivers; Performed by Order of the Government of the United States During the Years 1805, 1806, and 1807. And a Tour through the Interior Parts of New Spain when conducted through these Provinces by order of the Captain-General in the Year 1807.*

The book was so poorly prepared, so confused, that the publisher, in his own defense, added to the preface the footnote that he "owes it to truth . . . to state that he very much doubts whether any book ever went to press under so many disadvantages . . . Some of those disadvantages must be obvious . . . but there were many others . . . of sufficient magnitude to retard the work, embarrass the publisher, and impose more anxiety than has fallen to his lot in the various books he has published."

Pike made no money on the book. He wrote to Secretary of War Dearborn that he had allowed Conrad " . . . 20 pr. Cent on all sales" and that he, Pike, must "pay besides the expenses of printing &c. This, with bad debts and other Casualties will leave to myself an extreame small profit but as a soldiers views are more generally directed to fame than interest I hope that one object will at least be accomplished."

Some eighty years after Pike's death, Elliott Coues, who edited *The Journals of Lewis and Clark,* took up the monumental task of giving to the world a thorough study of Pike's explorations and espionage operations. In 1895, under the imprint of Francis P. Harper of New York, he published, in three volumes, *The Expeditions of Zebulon Montgomery Pike.*

To the original edition of Pike's *Account,* Coues appended explanatory footnotes that in themselves would have comprised an immense book. He included biographies of virtually every person Pike mentioned. He traced Pike's routes, described localities, Indian tribes, forts, towns, trading posts, identified flora and fauna, and included the history of events that were related in any way with Pike's career.

Coues made amazingly few errors, and most of these were due not to his own carelessness or to erroneous interpretations but to the fact that he was laboring under at least one severe handicap. The papers, notes, letters, and maps taken from Pike in Chihuahua, as well as Spanish documents pertaining to Pike's western expedition, were not available to him.

In the years immediately following the appearance of Coues's exhaustive work, attempts were made to locate the missing Pike papers, but to no avail.

However, in 1907, the noted historian, Herbert Eugene Bolton, was working in the Archives of Mexico when he came unexpectedly upon Pike's papers, as well as many of the Spanish documents relating to the Pike expedition to interior provinces of Spain. Bolton printed some of them in the *American Historical Review* in 1907 and 1908.

In 1910, the Mexican government acceded to the request of the American government that the papers be presented to the United States. When the papers were received in Washington, they were placed in the files of the War Department.

When, several years ago, Donald Jackson, who had edited numerous historical journals and documents, began work on a new edition of *The Journals of Zebulon Montgomery Pike*, these papers were made available to him. But Jackson had set for himself a goal far beyond their scope. He went to the files of the State Department, to the Archives of both the United States and Mexico, to museums, historical societies, Pike's descendants and private collectors, to the papers of Presidents Washington, Jefferson, Madison, and Monroe, as well as to the depositories of official military records. He traveled by land and by air over virtually every mile of Pike's routes in the United States and Mexico. He uncovered unpublished manuscript material and letters that threw new light on his subject. Jackson came up with facts never before revealed, and, as he stated, he treated every document "whether published or not, as raw material to be annotated and arranged without regard to the original edition." The letters that Pike printed "appear side by side with those he did not." In 1965, the University of Oklahoma Press published Jackson's work in two volumes.

Jackson gave new significance to the history of Pike. His research was exhaustive, his editing outstanding, his annotations and his arrangements clear, concise, and excellent. He did a superb job.

But the works of both Coues and Jackson, while they are distinguished contributions to history and belong in every public library, are for scholars. They were not written for the general reader, the person who enjoys history told in an uncomplicated manner, although accurate in detail, the person who prefers historical drama unburdened by footnotes and asides and appendices.

This is the type of story that I have tried to present —a story for the general reader who is not concerned with sources and references but who wants assurance that what he is reading is true.

For the student who wishes to delve deeper into the history of Pike, I offer as a guide the following selected bibliography.

ABERNATHY, THOMAS P.: *The Burr Conspiracy*, Oxford University Press, New York, 1954.

ADAMS, ALVA: *The Louisiana Purchase and Its First Explorer, Zebulon Montgomery Pike*, Colorado Springs, Colo., 1894.

ADAMS, HENRY: "The Burr Conspiracy," in *History of the United States*, Charles Scribner's Sons, New York, 1890, Vol. III.

BANCROFT, HUBERT HOWE: *History of Mexico*, Bancroft Co., San Francisco, 1886.

BENNET, ROBERT AMES: *A Volunteer with Pike*, Chicago, 1909. (A novel, purported to be based on the love of Dr. Robinson for a Mexican senorita.)

BIERCK, HAROLD A.: "Dr. John Hamilton Robinson," *Louisiana Historical Quarterly*, Vol. 25, pp. 644–669, 1942.

CALLAHAN, JAMES MORTON: *American Foreign Policy in Mexican Relations*, The Macmillan Company, New York, 1932.

CARTER, CLARENCE E.: "The Burr-Wilkinson Intrigue in St. Louis," *Missouri Historical Society Bulletin*, Vol. 10, pp. 447–464, 1910.

COX, ISAAC JOSLIN: "Wilkinson's Intrigues," *Encyclopaedia Britannica, Inc.*, Chicago (11th ed.), vol. 28.

CHRICHTON, KYLE S.: "Zeb Pike," *Scribner's*, vol. 82, pp. 462–467, 1927.

GREELY, GENERAL A. W.: *Explorers and Travellers*, Charles Scribner's Sons, New York, 1893.

HART, STEPHEN HARDING, and ARCHER BUTLER HULBERT: *Zebulon Pike's Arkansaw Journal*, The Denver Public Library, Denver, Colo., 1932.

HAVIGHURST, WALTER: *Upper Mississippi*, Farrar & Rinehart, Inc., New York, 1944.

HEITMAN, F. B.: *Historical Register of the United States Army*, Washington, 1890.

HOLLON, W. EUGENE: *The Lost Pathfinder: Zebulon Montgomery Pike*, University of Oklahoma Press, Norman, Okla., 1949.

HORGAN, PAUL: *Great River: The Rio Grande in North American History*, 2 vols., Rinehart & Company, Inc., New York, 1954.

HOUCK, LOUIS: *A History of Missouri,* 3 vols., R. R. Donnelley & Sons Company, Chicago, 1908.

JACOBS, JAMES RIPLEY: *Tarnished Warrior,* The Macmillan Company, New York, 1938.

————: *The Beginning of the U.S. Army, 1783–1812,* Princeton University Press, Princeton, N.J., 1947.

JACKSON, DONALD: "How Lost Was Zebulon Pike?," *American Heritage,* Vol. 16, pp. 10-15, 75-80, 1965.

JENKINSON, I.: *Aaron Burr,* Richmond, Ind., 1902.

MC CALEB, WALTER FLAVIUS: *The Aaron Burr Conspiracy,* Dodd, Mead & Company, Inc., New York, 1903.

MELINE, COL. JAMES F.: *Two Thousand Miles on Horseback,* Herd and Houghton, New York, 1867.

MOORHEAD, MAX L.: *New Mexico's Royal Road,* University of Oklahoma Press Norman, Okla., 1958.

OGLESBY, RICHARD E.: *Manuel Lisa and the Opening of the Missouri Fur Trade,* University of Oklahoma Press, Norman, Okla., 1963.

PARTON, JAMES: *The Life and Times of Aaron Burr,* 2 vols., Houghton Mifflin Company, Boston, 1892.

PEREZ DE VILLAGRA, GASPAR: *History of New Mexico,* trans. Gilberto Espinoza, notes by Frederick W. Hodge, Los Angeles, 1933.

PRENTIS, NOBLE L.: *Pike of Pike's Peak,* Topeka, 1878.

RICHARDSON, JAMES D.: *Messages and Papers of the Presidents,* 20 vols., 1789–1897, published by the authority of Congress, Washington, 1898.

SHEPHERD, W. R.: "Wilkinson and the Beginning of the Spanish Conspiracy," *American Historical Review,* vol. IX, 1904.

[247]

SPRAGUE, MARSHALL: *The Great Gates*, Little, Brown and Company, Boston, 1964.

TWITCHELL, RALPH EMERSON: *The Leading Facts of New Mexican History*, 2 vols., The Torch Press, Cedar Rapids, Iowa, 1912.
———: *Old Santa Fe*, Sante Fe, 1925.
———: *The Spanish Archives of New Mexico*, 2 vols., The Torch Press, Cedar Rapids, Iowa, 1914.

WILKINSON, JAMES: *Memoirs of My Own Times*, 3 vols., Philadelphia, Pa., 1816. (As dishonest as General Wilkinson's life.)

INDEX

DATE DUE